Question: Who is Ralph Storer?

Answer: Ralph was born in England about 50 metres from where Julius Caesar landed in 55 BC (Note: to dispel any ambiguity here – 55 BC was the date Julius landed; Ralph was born slightly later). He has walked and climbed extensively in the UK and around the world, and now lives in Scotland within reach of the Highlands. He is well known as a writer of hillwalking books, including the standard Scottish guidebooks *100 Best Routes on Scottish Mountains, The Ultimate Guide to the Munros* series and *Baffies' Easy Munro Guide* series.

Praise for *Mountain Trivia Quiz Challenge* American edition

A delightful collection of questions... Storer has managed to mix great enjoyment and intellectual stimulation in one small book... It will offer you hours of fun and information.
KLCC NATIONAL PUBLIC RADIO

A clever and informative quiz book... [it] deserves an honoured place in the bathroom-reading hall of fame as well as its very own backpack pocket.
SNOW COUNTRY

It's great fun for everyone, whether at a campfire in the great outdoors or waiting for traffic to move during the five o'clock rush hour.
ABILENE REPORTER

Praise for *Baffies Easy Munro Guide* series

Within the covers of this slim volume is a truly outstanding guidebook.
UNDISCOVERED SCOTLAND

...packed to bursting with concise information and route descriptions. There should be room for this guide in every couch potato's rucksack.
OUTDOOR WRITERS & PHOTOGRAPHERS GUILD

Praise for *The Ultimate Guide to the Munros* series

Fabulously illustrated...Entertaining as well as informative... One of the definitive guides to the Munros. PRESS & JOURNAL

Picks up where others – including my own – leave off, with lots of nitty-gritty information, all in a very up-beat style.
CAMERON MCNEISH

Brilliant. OUTDOOR WRITERS & PHOTOGRAPHERS GUILD

This is a truly indispensible guide for the Munro-bagger. Bursting with information, wit and a delightful irreverence. An absolute gem!
ALEX MACKINNON, Manager, Waterstone's George Street, Edinburgh

The ideal hillwalking companion. SCOTS MAGAZINE

His books are exceptional... Storer subverts the guidebook genre completely. THE ANGRY CORRIE

By the same author

100 Best Routes on Scottish Mountains (Little Brown)
50 Classic Routes on Scottish Mountains (Luath Press)
50 Best Routes on Skye and Raasay (Birlinn)
Exploring Scottish Hill Tracks (Little Brown)
The Joy of Hillwalking (Luath Press)
The Ultimate Guide to the Munros series:
   Volume 1: Southern Highlands
   Volume 2: Central Highlands South (including Glen Coe)
   Volume 3: Central Highlands North (including Ben Nevis)
   Volume 4: Cairngorms South (including Lochnagar)
Baffies' Easy Munro Guide series:
   Volume 1: Southern Highlands
   Volume 2: Central Highlands

The Ultimate Mountain Trivia Quiz Challenge

Volume I

RALPH STORER

Boot-tested and compiled by
The Go-Take-a-Hike Mountaineering Club

Luath Press Limited
EDINBURGH
www.luath.co.uk

Trifles make perfection, and perfection is no trifle.

Dedicated to others who seek answers to their questions

First published 2014
Reprinted 2014

ISBN: 978-1-908373-82-3

Printed and bound by
Bell & Bain Ltd., Glasgow

Typeset in 9.5 point Sabon and Frutiger

Contents

POT POURRI

Go-Take-A-Hike Mountaineering Club Committee

Ralph Storer President
Compiler of routes, penner of words, stopper of bucks, all-round good egg.

GiGi Custodian of the Common Sense

Farer (fairer?) of the Ways, arbiter of disputes, friend to all. Named after the two embarrassing grooves occasioned by too much fence-sitting.

F-Stop Controller of the Camera

Advisor of the Aperture. Recorder of the Ridiculous. So-named because he's always f***ing stopping to take photographs.

Needlepoint Companion of the Compass

Wary Watcher of the Weather. Finds featureless plateaus intimidating, doesn't understand GPS, barely understands a compass.

Chilly Willy Keeper of the Cool

AKA Snowballs. Peely-wally, estivates during summer, has never seen a midge, likes his toast crisp and even.

Torpedo Expender of the Energy

Bald and streamlined. Loather of laziness. Scorch marks on boots. Ascends as fast as a falling Munro-bagger descends.

Terminator   Raveller of the Rope

Grizzled, monosyllabic, self-taught suicide
commando. Hater of the horizontal. Measures
his life in scars.

Baffies   Entertainments Convenor

Allergic to exertion, prone to lassitude, suffers
from altitude sickness above 600m, blisters easily,
bleeds readily.

Introduction

THIS IS A QUIZ BOOK for people who love mountains and all things associated with them.

That means you.

How do we know this? Because if you were not interested in mountains, you wouldn't be reading this.

Okay, so right now you'd sooner be climbing a mountain. Who wouldn't? Unfortunately, there are times when it's not possible and that's where *The Ultimate Mountain Trivia Quiz Challenge* comes in.

When storm clouds sweep the summits and gales lash the flysheet, take time out and curl up in your sleeping bag with this book. When the days grow short and winter hail rattles against the window pane, put your feet up beside the fire and let this book take you in spirit to the mountains. When the summer sun beats down and induces lethargy, when the car journey to the trailhead seems to go on forever, when you're commuting to work and the long hard day stretches ahead and you wish you were in the mountains, let this book exercise your mind. Prepare yourself for the ultimate mountain challenge – the Mountain Trivia Quiz Challenge!

No matter whether you climb the fiercest faces in the depths of winter or take a short stroll to the mountain foot on a warm afternoon simply to stand and stare, this book is for you. Here you will find, grouped into 50 topics/quizzes, a smorgasbord of mountain-related questions. Some will enable you to show off your knowledge. Others will enable you to display your ignorance. Some are easy and satisfying, some are harder and more informative, some are curious and interesting. Some will stir your imagination, others will infuriate. Some answers you will know, some you won't, some you'll think you know but don't, some you'll think you don't know but do.

And there are yet others you may not wish to know.

The quizzes were devised by the committee of the Go-Take-a-Hike Mountaineering Club. We are an eclectic bunch and the quizzes reflect a wide range of interests and abilities, ranging geographically from the UK to Europe and the rest of the world. In addition, five committee members have each been leaned on to supply a couple of questions that reflect their particular interests, and there are a further eight *pot pourri* quizzes on topics both familiar and esoteric.

Of course, we realise that some questions may lie outside your realm of expertise and require 'informed guesswork', so we deign sometimes to offer clues or a range of possible answers. You're welcome. Ironically, it is often the topics you *don't* know that are the most interesting and fun to tackle. Hopefully they will provide as much pleasurable exercise for the mind as mountains do for the body. If you really want to get in the mood, lace up your boots, shoulder your pack and break out the Kendal mint cake. Before tackling a difficult question it might even be worth roping up and putting the first aid kit on standby... just in case.

How you tackle this book is up to you. It's as suitable for solitary quiz-surfing as it is for head-to-head combat with a rival or as a team game. Scoring is also a matter of personal choice. We suggest two points per correct answer. This will enable you to award yourself one point for a partially or nearly correct answer.

We have done our best to ensure that all answers are correct at time of writing, but a few may be open to minor dispute. Estimates of the heights of mountains, for instance, vary according to measurement method. A question on 'sea cliffs' presupposes an agreed definition of both sea (does a fjord count?) and cliff (how steep does a slope have to be to be called a cliff?). In the light of this, we abrogate any and all liability for injury or damage arising directly or indirectly from altercations concerning the accuracy of any and all information presented herein.

Finally, a word of warning. Quiz-surfing can be addictive. Certain committee members are still unable to climb a mountain or read a mountaineering book without potential questions forming unbidden in their minds. That way lies madness. There are more mountains than you will ever climb and more questions than you will ever answer. Climb and surf responsibly.

Ralph Storer
President, Go-Take-a-Hike M. C.

Beginner's Lucky Seven

If you can't answer these, give up now!

1. Arrange the following characters to spell the name of an 8000m Himalayan peak: 2K.

2. After which mountain are the Cairngorms named?

3. Who wrote the classic 1930s book on Alpine climbing entitled *Gervasutti's Climbs*?

4. In which country is Mount Kenya situated?

5. After whom is California's John Muir Trail named?

6. Which mountain range was the subject of Edward Whymper's 1891 classic mountaineering book *Travels Amongst the Great Andes of the Equator*?

7. How often is the annual Alpine Journal published?

Scottish Munros

1   Munros: General

A Munro is a separate mountain of 3000ft (914m) or over, as defined by Sir Hugh Munro and listed in Munro's Tables (1891 and later revised editions). A Top is a (nearby) mountain of 3000ft or over but one that is not sufficiently separated from the Munro to be considered a Munro itself.

1. The 282 Munros in Scotland are traditionally grouped for hill-walking and guidebook purposes into six regions. As of 2014, which of these regions contains the most Munros?

The Southern Highlands

The Central Highlands

The Cairngorms

The Western Highlands

The Northern Highlands

The Islands

2. Which of the six regions contains the most 4000ft (1220m) Munros?

3. How many Munros are higher than 1000m/3281ft?

    (a)   137
    (b)   174
    (c)   203

4. Name the only Scottish island apart from Skye that has any Munros.

5. Which of the following is the most common Munro name, with four occurrences (using variant spellings)?

    (a) Ben More
    (b) Carn Dearg
    (c) Geal Charn

6. In an alphabetical list of Munros, which comes first?

7. In 1984, following resurveying, a mountain was elevated to Munro status. In 2009, it was re-measured again at 914.6m/3000.80ft. Since then, it has overtaken (undertaken?) Ben Vane, re-measured at 915.76m/3004.60ft, as the lowest Munro of all. Name the mountain.

8. Since the last major (1997) revision of Munro's Tables, three Munros hold the record for having the most number of subsidiary Tops (five). Which Munro holds the historic record, having had nine subsidiary Tops from 1921 to 1981?

    (a) An Teallach
    (b) Cairn Gorm
    (c) Lochnagar

9. Who is generally recognised as being the first person to climb all the Munros?

    (a) A.E. Robertson
    (b) Hugh Munro
    (c) W.W. Naismith

10. As of 2014, how many Tops are there?

    (a) 226
    (b) 256
    (c) 286

2 Munros: The Southern Highlands

1. Which of these mountains is the most southerly Munro in Scotland?

   (a) Ben Lomond
   (b) Beinn Narnain
   (c) Stuc a' Chroin

2. *En route* to which Munro does an approach from Tyndrum pass a gold mine?

3. After what or whom is Crianlarich's An Caisteal, meaning The Castle, named?

   (a) A castellated rock formation on the north ridge
   (b) A summit outcrop shaped like a chess piece
   (c) Glenfalloch Castle at its foot

4. Which of these Munros is the highest summit south of Ben Nevis?

   (a) Ben Lawers
   (b) Ben More
   (c) Stob Binnein

5. Which popular Munro was formerly known as Maiden's Pap on account of its shape?

   (a) Beinn Dorain
   (b) Ben Vane
   (c) Schiehallion

6. Bypassing intermediate highpoints, which Southern Highlands Munro requires the least ascent from a public road?

   (a) Beinn Heasgarnich (1078m/3536ft) from the Glen Lochay-Glen Lyon road
   (b) Meall Buidhe (932m/3058ft) from the Loch an Daimh road
   (c) Meall nan Tarmachan (1044m/3425ft) from the Lochan na Lairige road

7. After what or whom is Ben Challum named?

    (a) Calumny
    (b) Columbine
    (c) St Columba

8. Beginning at the foot of the mountain at Rowardennan, the Ben Lomond hill race (up and down) is 7.5ml/12km long and involves 970m/3700ft of ascent. What is the record finishing time?

    (a) 1 hour 5 minutes 51 seconds
    (b) 1 hour 29 minutes 37 seconds
    (c) 1 hour 58 minutes 13 seconds

9. Ben Vorlich can be climbed easily from the A82 south of Crianlarich or the A84 north of Callander, even though the roads are more than 15ml/24km apart as the eagle flies. How is this possible?

10. Why is Lochan na Cat in the Lawers Range so named?

    (a) The area was once well known for its wild cats
    (b) The lochan is shaped like a sitting cat
    (c) The lochan's reeds were formerly woven into whips for the herding of cattle

3   Munros: The Central Highlands

1. Which of these mountains, overlooking a west coast sea loch, is the most westerly Munro in the Central Highlands?

    (a)   Ben Cruachan
    (b)   Beinn Sgulaird
    (c)   Sgorr Dhonuill (of Beinn a' Bheithir)

2. The Gaelic name of Meall a' Bhuiridh (1108m/3635ft) at the head of Glen Coe means Hill of Roaring. Roaring of what?

    (a)   Deer
    (b)   Waterfalls
    (c)   Wind

3. On the slopes of which Munro in upper Glen Nevis is An Steall (The Waterfall), whose 110m/350ft drop makes it the third highest in Scotland?

    (a)   An Gearanach
    (b)   Stob Ban
    (c)   Sgurr a' Mhaim

4. Name the Central Highlands Munro that would have a railway to its summit had an 1893 proposal been implemented.

    (a)   Aonach Mor (Spean Bridge)
    (b)   Ben Nevis (Fort William)
    (c)   Sgairneach Mhor (Drumochter Pass)

5. Which of these Glen Coe mountains did NOT have its Munro tally doubled by the last major (1997) revision of Munro's Tables?

    (a)   Aonach Eagach
    (b)   Buachaille Etive Beag
    (c)   Buachaille Etive Mor
    (d)   Bidean nam Bian

6. Name the mountain range in miniature whose two Munros enclose a reservoir-filled corrie and a massive cavern excavated to house a hydro-electric scheme machine room, as a result of which the mountain is sometimes called the 'Hollow Mountain'.

7. Name the 937m/3074ft west coast Munro whose Gaelic name, deriving from the mountain's shape, means The Hat-shaped Mountain.

   (a) Beinn Fhionnlaidh
   (b) Beinn Sgulaird
   (c) Sgorr Dhonuill

8. Name the Munro that, uniquely in Scotland, is easier to reach by railway than by public road.

9. Two mountains in the Central Highlands are called Am Bodach, meaning The Old Man. One is a Munro in the Mamores. The other is a Top of which Munro?

   (a) Creag Meagaidh (Glen Spean)
   (b) Meall Dearg (Glen Coe)
   (c) Ben Starav (Glen Etive)

10. Of the 73 Munros in the Central Highlands, 42 are named Ben/ Beinn, Sgurr/Sgor/Sgorr or Stob. Which are there more of: Bens, Sgurrs or Stobs?

4 Munros: The Cairngorms

1. Which of these mountains is the most easterly Munro in Scotland?

   (a) Ben Avon
   (b) Morven
   (c) Mount Keen

2. The Cairngorms are divided into northern and southern regions by a great corridor that bisects the region from west to east, beginning as Glen Feshie and running through Braemar and along the Dee Valley to the North Sea coast. All the 1220m/4000ft peaks lie north of this line. What is the highest mountain south of it?

3. Bypassing intermediate highpoints, which Cairngorms Munro requires the least ascent from a public road?

   (a) A' Bhuidheanach Bheag (936m/3071ft) from Drumochter Pass
   (b) Cairn Gorm (1244m/4081ft) from Coire Cas car park
   (c) The Cairnwell (933m/3061ft) from the Cairnwell Pass

4. At the Cairnwell Pass at head of Glen Shee, a vehicle track connects the summits of The Cairnwell and Carn Aosda. Name the only other (nearby) Munro that has a vehicle track all the way to its 1051m/3448ft summit.

5. Which Munro south of Braemar has aircraft wreckage on its summit plateau?

   (a) Carn a' Choire Bhoidheach
   (b) Carn an t-Sagairt Mor
   (c) Cairn Bannoch

6. From the original 1891 edition of Munro's Tables to the 1981 revision, there were five Munros on the plateau above Glen Feshie. How many are there now?

7. Which of the three major Cairngorms Plateaus is the source of the River Dee?

    (a) The Western Cairngorms Plateau between Braeriach and Sgor an Lochain Uaine
    (b) The Central Cairngorms Plateau between Cairn Gorm and Ben Macdui
    (c) The Eastern Cairngorms Plateau between Ben a' Bhuird and Ben Avon

8. Name the Cairngorm Munro that is Scotland's own Table Mountain, with a summit plateau so flat that for a whole 2ml/3km it doesn't vary in height more than a few tens of metres.

9. Before 1810, which Cairngorms mountain was thought to be the highest in Scotland?

    (a) Ben Macdui
    (b) Braeriach
    (c) Cairn Gorm

10. Which of the three Munros in Question 9 is said to be haunted by Am Fear Liath Mor (The Big Grey Man), a malevolent spectral apparition with whom several distinguished mountaineers have had spine-chilling encounters in swirling cloud?

5 Munros: The Western Highlands

1. Which of these mountains is the most westerly Munro on the mainland of Scotland?

    (a) Beinn Sgritheall (Loch Hourn)
    (b) Ladhar Bheinn (Knoydart)
    (c) Tom na Gruagaich (of Beinn Alligin, Torridon)

2. Name the 1040m/3413ft Munro known as the 'Matterhorn of the Western Highlands'.

3. Which of these Munros is the highest mountain in Scotland north of the Great Glen, which links Fort William to Inverness?

    (a) Carn Eighe (Glen Affric)
    (b) Sgurr Fiona (of An Teallach, Dundonnell)
    (c) Spidean a' Choire Leith (of Liathach, Torridon)

4. Which 974m/3195ft west coast Munro has one of the longest and steepest continuous slopes in Britain, its summit being only 1ml/1.6km north of a sea loch?

5. Name the Western Highlands Munro that, following GPS satellite re-measurement in 2009, was found to be less than 3000ft high, thereby reducing the then number of Munros from 284 to 283.

    (a) Beinn Fhionnlaidh
    (b) Carn Eighe
    (c) Sgurr nan Ceannaichean

6. Which Western Highlands Munro has five satellite Tops, making it tie with two other Munros for having the most number of Tops?

    (a) Mam Sodhail, Glen Affric
    (b) Sgurr nan Ceathreamhnan, Glen Affric
    (c) The Saddle, Glen Shiel

7. Which 1032m/3385ft Munro will you circumnavigate if you begin on the west coast at Loch Duich, walk eastwards through Gleann Lichd to Alltbeithe youth hostel and return via the Bealach an Sgairne pass?

8. Name the Munro whose easy northern access was cut off by the building of Loch Mullardoch reservoir in 1951. The normal access route now approaches from the south over the summit of another Munro.

   (a) Beinn Fhionnlaidh
   (b) Carn Eighe
   (c) Toll Creagach

9. On the slopes of which 918m/3011ft Munro are the Falls of Glomach, which by some estimates are the highest in Scotland?

10. Which of these Torridon mountains did NOT have its Munro tally doubled by the last major (1997) revision of Munro's Tables?

   (a) Beinn Alligin
   (b) Beinn Eighe
   (c) Liathach

6   Munros: The Northern Highlands

1. Which of these mountains is the most northerly Munro in Scotland?

    (a)   Ben Hope
    (b)   Ben Klibreck
    (c)   Ben Loyal

2. Which of these Munros is the highest mountain in the Northern Highlands?

    (a)   Beinn Dearg (near Ullapool)
    (b)   Spidean a' Choire Leith (of Liathach, Torridon)
    (c)   Sgurr Mor (Fannichs)

3. Name the Northern Highlands Munro that, following GPS satellite re-measurement in 2011, was found to be less than 3000ft high, resulting in the then number of Munros being reduced from 283 to 282 in 2012.

    (a)   Beinn a' Chlaidheimh
    (b)   Beinn Damh
    (c)   Beinn Tarsuinn

4. Name the Munro whose late-lying snow traditionally made it possible for the MacKenzie Earls of Cromarty to rent their land from the Crown on condition that they could produce a snowball at any time of year. The proximity of Inverness has given rise to recurrent proposals for downhill ski development on the mountain's slopes.

5. The mountains of the Northern Highlands are partly formed from the most ancient rocks in Europe – Lewissian gneiss up to 3000 million years old. In 2004, this resulted in the creation of Scotland's first... what?

    (a)   Geological Museum
    (b)   Geological Park
    (c)   National Park

6. Which Northern Highlands mountain has the most summits in Munro's Tables, with two Munros and seven Tops?

    (a)   An Teallach
    (b)   Beinn Eighe
    (c)   Liathach

7. Which compact Northern Highlands group of nine Munros is named after a loch on its southern perimeter?

8. Name the isolated Northern Highlands Munro distinctive for its two-tiered structure, with a plinth of ice-scoured Lewissian gneiss topped by a craggy summit of Torridonian sandstone. Popular as a calendar picture, its Gaelic name means The Spear.

9. Which Torridon Munro did NOT have its Munro tally doubled by the last major (1997) revision of Munro's Tables?

    (a)   Beinn Alligin
    (b)   Beinn Eighe
    (c)   Liathach

10. Name the 987m/3238ft Northern Highlands Munro that is the only Munro in Scotland whose standard ascent route passes limestone caves.

    (a)   Ben Klibreck
    (b)   Conival
    (c)   Seana Bhraigh

7 Munros: Ben Nevis

1. Which of the following is NOT one of the four classic north face ridges of Ben Nevis?
   (a) Castle Ridge
   (b) Pinnacle Ridge
   (c) Tower Ridge
   (d) North-East Buttress

2. The corrie on the north side of Ben Nevis, at the foot of the north face, is called Coire Leis. Why is the ridge around the head of the corrie called the CMD Arête?

3. Approximately how much more rain is there at the top of Ben Nevis than at the bottom?
   (a) Twice as much
   (b) Three times as much
   (c) Four times as much

4. What is the average number of daily hours of sunshine at the summit of Ben Nevis?
   (a) Two hours
   (b) Four hours
   (c) Six hours

5. After which Scottish Mountaineering Club member and pioneering north face climber was the SMC hut in Coire Leis named?
   (a) Norman Collie
   (b) Harold Raeburn
   (c) Charles Inglis Clark

6. The maximum depth of snow recorded at the summit of Ben Nevis occurred in 1885. How deep was it?
   (a) 71ins/180cm
   (b) 142ins/360cm
   (c) 213ins/540cm

7. On 14 September 1909, Miss Elizabeth Wilson-Smith set a new record time of 1 hour 51 minutes for the ascent of Ben Nevis. Why was her record not officially recognised?

   (a) Because cloud cover caused her to turn back at a cairn 100m before the true summit
   (b) Because no-one believed her at the time
   (c) Because she was a woman

8. Why is the classic 1954 north face rock climb Sassenach so called?

   (a) It was first climbed on St George's Day
   (b) It was first climbed by two Scotsmen, who named it disparagingly after finding it easier than expected
   (c) It was first climbed by two Englishmen, who named it after hearing an envious cry of 'English bastards!'

9. The summit of Ben Nevis was sold in 2000. To which body?

   (a) John Muir Trust
   (b) Scottish Natural Heritage
   (c) National Trust for Scotland

10. Why have more Chinese people climbed Ben Nevis since 1997?

8 Munros: History

1. The first recorded ascent of a Munro was by Colin 'The Mad' Campbell in 1590. Which Munro did he climb?

   (a) Ben Wyvis
   (b) Mount Keen
   (c) Stuchd an Lochain

2. The second recorded ascent of a Munro was by Londoner John Taylor, the 'Water Poet', in 1611. Which of the three Munros in Question 1 did he climb?

3. Why did James Robertson make the first recorded ascent of Ben Nevis in 1771?

   (a) To make meteorological observations
   (b) To search for botanical specimens
   (c) For a bet

4. There was an observatory on the summit of Ben Nevis from 1883–1904. What was its purpose?

   (a) To make astronomical observations
   (b) To make geophysical observations
   (c) To make meteorological observations

5. Where was Scotland's first skiers' hut built in 1932?

   (a) Ben Lawers (Coire Odhar)
   (b) Cairn Gorm (Coire Cas)
   (c) Meall a' Bhuiridh (Glen Coe)
   (d) The Cairnwell (Glen Shee)

6. On which of the Munros in Question 5 was Scotland's first permanent ski tow built in 1956?

7. Which 1214m/3983ft Munro was, until re-measurement in 1852, thought to exceed the 4000ft mark? In 1878 a 6m/20ft cairn was erected on the summit to 'restore' its height, and in 1879 it became Sir Hugh Munro's first recorded ascent at the age of 23.

8. Why did the Astronomer Royal Nevil Maskelyne spend four months on Schiehallion in 1774?

    (a) To estimate the mass of the earth
    (b) To observe Halley's Comet
    (c) To observe the Transit of Venus

9. Which Munro prompted surveyor Charles Hutton to invent contour lines?

    (a) Ben Challum
    (b) The Cairnwell
    (c) Schiehallion

10. Name the first of many Cairngorm Munros climbed by Queen Victoria (mostly on the back of a pony). The year was 1844, she was 25 years old and she was staying at Blair Castle in Blair Atholl.

    (a) Carn a' Chlamain
    (b) Carn Liath (of Beinn a' Ghlo)
    (c) Beinn Dearg

9 Munros: Odd One Out

In each of the following ten lists of Munros, one of the four items is different from the other three. With the help of the clues given, can you find it?

1. Cairnwell   Devil's Point
   Saddle   Bannoch
   Clue: The Definite Article

2. Sgurr a' Ghreadaidh   Sgurr a' Mhadaidh
   Sgurr Alasdair   Sgurr Mhor
   Clue: The Cuillin

3. Cairn Gorm   Glas Maol
   Glas Tulaichean   Meall a' Bhuiridh
   Clue: Ski lifts

4. Ladhar Bheinn   Luinne Bheinn
   Lurg Mhor   Meall Buidhe
   Clue: Knoydart

5. Aonach (Glen Spean)   Binnein (Mamores)
   Bynack (Cairngorms)   Monadh (Cairngorms)
   Clue: Mor/More + Beag/Beg (Big + Little)

6. Sgurr na Carnach   Sgurr na Ciste Duibhe
   Sgurr nan Conbhairean   Sgurr Fhuaran
   Clue: Five Sisters

7. Ben Avon (Cairngorms)   Beinn Mheadhoin (Cairngorms)
   Gulvain (Morar)   Sgurr nan Gillean (Skye)
   Clue: Summit scrambles

8. Carn a' Chlamain (Glen Tilt)   Carn an Fhidhleir (Glen Geldie)
   Carn an Tuirc (Cairnwell)   Mullach Clach a' Bhlair (Glen Feshie)

   Clue: Vehicle tracks

9. Ben Avon   Ben Hope
   Ben Nevis   Ben Ossian
   Clue: Lochs

10. An Socach (Glen Affric)   An Socach (Glen Cannich)
    An Socach (Glen Ey)   An Socach (Glen Shiel)
    Clue: Snout (Socach) or Nowt

10 Munros: Anagrams

Can you find the names of the Munros hidden in the following
anagrams?

1. O BLOND MEN
    Clue: a popular Southern Highlands Munro (3,6)

2. CLEAR WHEN LIT
    Clue: a Glen Shee skiers' mountain (3,9)

3. MR ORGANIC
    Clue: a Cairngorms 'four-thousander' (5,4)

4. REBEL SWAN
    Clue: a Loch Tay Munro (3,6)

5. DUB CINEMA
    Clue: another Cairngorms 'four-thousander' (3,6)

6. SNUG CHIC REAR
    Clue: a pointy West Highlands peak (5,2,5)

7. BONZE NICHE
    Clue: A retiring Southern Highlands Munro (3,7)

8. EVIDENT HOT LIPS
    Clue: an iconic Cairngorms Munro (3,6,5)

9. MEN BORE
    Clue: a Southern Highlands Munro (3,4)

10. REAL BEND
    Clue: a remote Central Highlands Munro (3,5)

11. A LONG ARCH

Clue: a famous Cairngorms Munro (9)

12. OH LISA LICHEN

Clue: a much-photographed Southern Highlands Munro (12)

13. MERRY ARCING ROD

Clue: an unsung Cairngorms Munro (5,9)

14. EVEN NIBS

Clue: (you shouldn't need a clue) (3,5)

15. MARCIA EGGHEAD

Clue: a Loch Laggan Munro (5,7)

Scottish Highlands & Islands

11 Scottish Mountain and Hill Ranges

Name the following Scottish mountain and hill ranges.

1. A Central Highlands mountain range whose twisting main ridge contains four Munros. It is named after the quartzite slopes that drop from either side of the ridge.

2. In Gaelic, a mountain range that was formerly known as the Monadh Ruadh (Red Mountains) but whose English name now means the Blue Mountains.

    (a)   Aonachs
    (b)   Cairngorms
    (c)   Fannichs

3. Dark eminences on the edge of Rannoch Moor?

4. A compact group of hills north-east of Aviemore, high point Creagan a' Chaise (732m/2401ft), separating the valleys of the Spey and the Avon. A famous traditional Scottish song commemorates a battle fought on the range's slopes in 1690.

    (a)   Braes of Abernethy
    (b)   Hills of Cromdale
    (c)   Ladder Hills

5. A range with a grandiose name on the edge of the Scottish Highlands. It contains four Munros but its most striking peak is not a Munro.

6. A range of hills, high point 721m/2366ft, that rims the north side of the Forth Valley.

    (a)   Campsies
    (b)   Ochils
    (c)   Pentlands

7. A group of mountains on the opposite side of the Spey Valley to the Cairngorms, which had two of its six Munros deleted from Munro's Tables in 1981.

8. A range of bare rock peaks whose clutch of Munros tower above the Sea of the Hebrides.

   (a) Cuillin of Rum
   (b) Cuillin of Skye
   (c) Paps of Jura

9. A range of ten Munros whose white quartzite summits are often mistaken for snow-capped tops. Its name is Gaelic for 'Big Breasts'.

10. A group of hills, high point 732m/2402ft, which rise above the two highest villages in Scotland.

   (a) Ladder Hills
   (b) Lowther Hills
   (c) Moorfoot Hills

12 Scottish Corbetts

A Corbett is a Highland mountain with a height between 762m/ 2500ft and 914m/2999ft, as defined by J. Rooke Corbett and listed in Corbetts Tables (1921 and later revised editions). Name the following Corbetts.

1. The 874m/2867ft hill that is the highest of four Corbetts on the island of Arran.

2. The prominent mountain in the Arrochar Alps that was a Munro in the first (1891) edition of Munro's Tables, with a height of 3021ft (921m), but which was demoted to Corbett status in 1981 with a height of 901m/2956ft.

    (a)   Beinn an Lochain
    (b)   Ben Donich
    (c)   The Cobbler

3. The 799m/2621ft hill that is the highest point on the island of Harris and the only Corbett in the Outer Hebrides.

    (a)   Clisham
    (b)   Oreval
    (c)   Ullaval

4. The far north peak of shattered quartzite whose possible Munro status was debated throughout the twentieth century. The argument was settled by a 2007 survey that gave it a height of 911m/2988ft.

    (a)   Arkle
    (b)   Cranstackie
    (c)   Foinaven

5. The steep Torridon mountain whose 914m height almost makes it a Munro, but whose Corbett status was confirmed by a 2007 survey that gave it a height of 2997.58ft.

   (a) Baosbheinn
   (b) Beinn an Eoin
   (c) Beinn Dearg

6. The 785m/2575ft hill that is the highest of the three Paps of Jura and the only Corbett on the island.

   (a) Beinn a' Chaolais
   (b) Beinn an Oir
   (c) Beinn Shiantaidh

7. The 812m/2664ft hill that is the highest point on the island of Rum.

   (a) Ainshval
   (b) Askival
   (c) Hallival

8. The higher of the two conspicuous hills west of the A9 on approach to Drumochter Pass north of Blair Atholl. The lower hill (An Torc in Gaelic) is known as the Boar of Badenoch (739m/2424ft). The Gaelic name of the higher hill is Meall an Dobharchain (803m/2634ft).

9. The 839m/2752ft mountain at the foot of Glen Etive opposite Ben Starav, famous for the friction climbs on its 200m sweep of steep, overlapping slabs.

10. The multi-topped 764m/2506ft peak near Tongue on the north coast of Scotland, known from its picturesque appearance as the 'Queen of the Scottish Peaks'.

13 The Isle Of Skye

1. How many Munros are there on Skye?

    (a)   10
    (b)   12
    (c)   14

2. One Skye Munro in the original 1891 edition of the Tables was demoted to Top status in the 1921 edition and deleted from the Tables altogether in the latest (1997) edition. Name it.

    (a)   Sgurr Dearg
    (b)   Sgurr Sgumain
    (c)   Sgurr Thearlaich

3. Which Cuillin summit was controversially elevated to Top status in the latest (1997) edition of Munro's Tables?

    (a)   Bidein Druim nan Ramh
    (b)   Knight's Peak
    (c)   Sgurr Thuilm

4. Which Skye mountain was described in Gaelic by the 18th Century poet William Ross, known as the Gaelic Bard, as 'Queen of mountains fair though stern'?

    (a)   Bla Bheinn
    (b)   Sgurr Alasdair
    (c)   Sgurr nan Gillean

5. What disappeared from the west ridge of Sgurr nan Gillean in the winter of 1986–7?

    (a)   Its *gendarme* (rock tower)
    (b)   Its overhang
    (c)   The rock slab containing the etched initials of Alexander Nicolson from his first ascent in 1865

6. There are no Corbetts (individual 762m/2500ft hills) in the Cuillin, but how many are there elsewhere on Skye?

   (a) 2
   (b) 4
   (c) 6

7. Sleat in South Skye is the lowest of the island's five main peninsulas, with no hill reaching 300m/1000ft. With a height of 294m/965ft, which Sleat hill is the highest?

   (a) Sgiath-bheinn an Uird, near Ord
   (b) Sgurr na Caorach, near Point of Sleat
   (c) Sgurr na h-Iolaire, near Tarskavaig

8. By what name are Healabhal Mhor and Healabhal Bheag more commonly known?

   (a) MacLeod's Maidens
   (b) MacLeod's Tables
   (c) The Bonnets

9. Name the intimidatingly flaky rock pinnacle that was the subject of Victorian climber Harold Raeburn's famous throwaway remark: '(it) may be climbable but we didn't make an attempt'.

   (a) Kilt Rock
   (b) The Needle
   (c) The Old Man of Storr

10. Name Skye's most celebrated cave, described by Sir Walter Scott as 'Strathaird's enchanted cell'.

   (a) Candlestick Cave
   (b) Spar Cave
   (c) Uamh Oir (Cave of Gold)

14 Scottish Island Highpoints

Match each mountain or hill in List 1 with the Scottish island in List 2 of which it is the highest point.

List 1

1. An Sgurr (393m/1290ft)
2. Askival (812m/2665ft)
3. Beinn an Oir (785m/2576ft)
4. Ben Hough (119m/391ft)
5. Clisham (799m/2622ft)
6. Dun Caan (443m/1454ft)
7. Dun I (100m/328ft)
8. Goat Fell (874m/2868ft)
9. Heaval (383m/1257ft)
10. Mealisval (574m/1884ft)
11. Ward Hill (481m/1579ft)
12. Windy Hill (278m/913ft)

List 2

a. Arran
b. Barra
c. Bute
d. Eigg
e. Harris
f. Hoy
g. Iona
h. Jura
i. Lewis
j. Raasay
k. Rum.
l. Tiree

15 Scotland: What And Where?

The following mountain features are all found in the Scottish Highlands. What and where are they?

1. The Lost Valley

2. The Ring of Steall

3. The Barns of Bynack

4. The Executioner's Tooth

5. The Grey Mare's Tail

6. Lord Berkeley's Seat

7. The Tailors' Stone

8. The Witch's Step

9. The Bloody Stone

10. The Colonel's Bed

11. Argyll's Eyeglass

12. The Giant's Staircase

13. The Streak of Lightning

14. Cluny's Cage

15. The White Lady

16 Cryptic Scottish Mountains and Hills

Can you find the names of the Scottish mountains and hills hidden in the following cryptic clues?

1. A mixed up minor crag on Speyside? Hardly! (5,4)

2. Billy slipped on Arran. (8)

3. Little Benjamin and the solicitors are missing the Wye, at least it sounds like it on Tayside. (3,6)

4. An Angus Munro that dehydrates before it starts hotting up. (6)

5. A summit both to stride up and sit astride in the Western Highlands (3,6)

6. Ben and Arthur's collective name for a Southern Highlands Corbett. (3,7)

7. In the Central Highlands, little Alastair gets caught up in a drunken spree. (3,5)

8. Duncan is plodding up a bit of this Northern Highlands Corbett. (6)

9. An enthusiastic Cairngorms Munro. (5,4)

10. Coils back on first hard Northern Highlands Munro. (6)

11. Some massacre is evident in the Glen Coe area. (6)

12. A Great Glen Corbett that is both crooked and oddly even. (3,3)

13. Back parts surround ridge-end in the Western Highlands. (6)

14. A Cairngorms Munro made from month five and six months. (5)

15. A Northern Highlands Munro forged from all tea and boundless chance. (2,7)

England and Wales

17 English Mountains and Hills

Name the following English mountains and hills.

1. The most northerly 914m/3000ft mountain in England.

    (a) Blencathra (Saddleback)
    (b) Scafell Pike
    (c) Skiddaw

2. The highest hill in England outside the Lake District.

    (a) Cross Fell
    (b) Great Shunner Fell
    (c) The Cheviot

3. The most northerly 609m/2000ft hill in England, one of the three in Question 2.

4. The 320m/1050ft hill known as the 'Matterhorn of Cleveland'.

5. The highest of the Three Peaks in the Yorkshire Dales National Park.

    (a) Ingleborough
    (b) Pen-y-ghent
    (c) Whernside

6. The 621m/2037 hilltop that is the highest point south of Wales.

    (a) Brown Willy, Bodmin Moor
    (b) Dunkery Beacon, Exmoor
    (c) High Willhays, Dartmoor

7. The highest hilltop (103m/337ft) in the lowest English county.

    (a) Chrishall Common, Essex
    (b) Beacon Hill, Norfolk
    (c) Great Wood Hill, Suffolk

8. The 636m/2086ft hilltop that is the highest point in the Peak District.

9. The 517m/1696ft Peak District hill known as Shivering Mountain on account of its numerous landslips caused by unstable shale.

   (a) Giggleswick Scar
   (b) Gragareth
   (c) Mam Tor

10. The 228m/749ft hill known as England's 'first and last' because it is close to Land's End.

   (a) Brown Willy
   (b) Carn Brea
   (c) Goonhilly Downs

18 Welsh Mountains and Hills

1. How many Welsh peaks top 914m/3000ft?

2. Wales traditionally had four mountains with a height of
    1000m/3281ft or over. Resurveying by GPS satellite in 2010
    added a fifth. Which mountain?

    (a) Carnedd Daffyd
    (b) Crib y Ddysgl
    (c) Glyder Fawr

3. Name the 689m/2261ft hill known as 'The Matterhorn of North
    Wales'.

4. Which range of hills contains the highest peak in Britain south of
    Snowdonia?

    (a) The Arans, east of Dolgellau
    (b) The Arenigs, north-east of Dolgellau
    (c) The Nantlle Ridge, north-west of Dolgellau

5. Which 893m/2930ft mountain is named after the deep hollow of
    Cwm y Gadair on its northern flank, which supposedly made a
    chair for a legendary Welsh giant?

6. Name the shapely 872m/2861ft Snowdonia peak that dominates
    the southern view from Capel Curig.

    (a) Moel Hebog
    (b) Moel Siabod
    (c) Mynydd Mawr

7. Name the 752m/2468ft hill on whose slopes can be found the
    sources of both the Severn and the Wye, and whose ascent was
    described by an 1813 guidebook as 'a protracted bog walk'.

    (a) Mynydd Trawsnant
    (b) Plynlimon Fawr
    (c) Trawsallt

8. Which village in Snowdonia was described in an 1881 guidebook as 'the Chamonix of Wales'?

9. Name the 536m/1759ft hill that is the highest point in Pembrokeshire Coast National Park.

    (a) Foel Cwmcerwyn
    (b) Foel Drygarn
    (c) Foel Eryr

10. In the 1950s, Joe Brown and his colleagues made use of the Snowdon Mountain Railway to descend from near the summit of Snowdon after rock-climbing on the mountain. How did they accomplish their descent?

19 Mountain and Hill Ranges of England and Wales

Name the following mountain and hill ranges of England and Wales.

1. A range that contains more 914m/3000ft summits than any other range outside Scotland.

2. A range of limestone hills in south-west England, more famous for its gorges and caves than its tops.

   (a) Cambrians
   (b) Cheddar Hills
   (c) Mendips

3. A Welsh range named after its two highest summits, *Fawr* (Big; 1000m/3283ft) and *Fach* (Little; 994m/3261ft). The higher top is a stony plateau, while the lower top is a chaotic pile of slabs.

   (a) Carneddau
   (b) Glyders
   (c) Moelwyns

4. Another Welsh range named after its two highest summits, *Fawr* (720m/2363ft) and *Fach* (712m/2337ft). Despite its modest height, its ruggedness made it a training ground for 20th Century British Himalayan expeditions.

   (a) Black Mountains
   (b) Harlech Dome
   (c) Rhinogs

5. A group of craggy peaks above Stickle Tarn in the Lake District, named after the valley it dominates.

6. A range of gentle, wooded hills whose crest is followed by the 87ml/139km-long Ridgeway long distance trail, said to be the oldest road in Britain.

   (a) Chilterns
   (b) Cotswolds
   (c) Shropshire Downs

7. A range of rolling hills in south-west England, one of the three in Question 6. It is crossed by a 100ml/160km long distance trail (Way) named after them.

8. A Welsh range that contains the highest mountains south of Snowdonia.

9. A range that consists of a narrow 9ml/14km ridge of volcanic rock, where the massive prehistoric earthworks of British Camp cover 32 acres on the broad 339m/1114ft summit of Herefordshire Beacon.

10. A range that contains the highest mountains in South Wales.

20 British Island Highpoints

Match each hill in List 1 with the British island in List 2 of which it is the highest point.

List 1

1. Cliff top (off Northumberland) 19m/63ft
2. Hautnez 111m/365ft
3. Holyhead Mountain 220m/722ft
4. Le Moulin 114m/375ft
5. Le Rond 101m/332ft
6. Snaefell 621m/2038ft
7. St Boniface Down 241m/71ft
8. The Mount 76m/250ft
9. Unnamed (in Scilly Isles) 51m/168ft
10. Unnamed (off Devon north) 142m/466ft
11. Unnamed (off Devon south) 43m/142ft
12. Unnamed (off Pembrokeshire) 79m/260ft

List 2

a. Alderney
b. Anglesey
c. Guernsey
d. Inner Farne
e. Isle of Man
f. Isle of Sheppey
g. Isle of Wight
h. Lundy
i. Sark
j. Skomer
k. St Mary's
l. Thatcher Rock

21 Lake District: Odd One Out

In each of the following ten lists of Lake District features, one of the four items is different from the other three. With the help of the clues given, can you find it?

1. Black   Bleaberry
   Blind   Boo
   Clue: Tarns

2. Causey   Cofa
   Cold   Rosthwaite
   Clue: Pikes

3. Knott   Road
   Stile   Street
   Clue: Highs

4. Door   End
   Gable   Knott
   Clue: Greats

5. Broad Stand   Deep Gill
   Jack's Rake   Lord's Rake
   Clue: Scafell

6. Scandale Pass   Stake Pass
   Sticks Pass   Whinlatter Pass
   Clue: Roads

7. Haweswater   Hayeswater
   Kentmere   Wet Sleddale
   Clue: Reservoirs

8. Jackdaw Ridge   Longshoreman's Arête
   Sharp Edge   Wet Side Edge
   Clue: Scrambles

9. Greenburn   Long
   Warnscale   Wrynose

   Clue: Bottoms

10. Dow Crag   Pikes Crag
    Pulpit Rock   Walla Crag

    Clue: Scafell Pike

22   Lake District Hills: Anagrams

Can you find the names of the Lake District hills hidden in the following anagrams?

1. GARBLE GATE
    Clue: a 899m/2950ft hill above Wasdale (5,5)

2. CARNAL BETH
    Clue: a 868m/2848ft hill in the Northern Lake District (10)

3. WARM ETHEL
    Clue: a 763m/2502ft hill south of Wrynose Pass (9)

4. RON BISON
    Clue: a 829m/2720ft hill in the Buttermere Fells (8)

5. FERRET HALL
    Clue: the name of two Lake District hills, the higher in the east (778m/2553ft) and the lower in the west (649m/2130ft) (6,4)

6. LADYLIKE PONG OW
    Clue: a 858m/2816ft hill above Grisedale Tarn (10,4)

7. SPLICE FLAKE
    Clue: a pre-eminent 978m/3210ft Lake District hill (7,4)

8. TERSE THIGH
    Clue: a 828m/2717ft hill above Blea Water (4,6)

9. RICH LIKE TORN ASS
    A 736m/2415ft hill west of Grasmere (8,7)

10. TACKY SASH
    Clue: a 597m/1959ft hill above Warnscale Bottom (9)

11. MOON IN SCOTLAND

   Clue: a 803m/2635ft hill named after one of the lakes (8,3,3)

12. WEARY BROW

   Clue: a 627m/2058ft hill above Wast Water (9)

13. WISE EDITH

   Clue: a 707m/2320ft hill near Crummock Water (9)

14. MILL GLEN

   Clue: a 807m/2609ft hill north of Scafell Pike (8)

15. MEL BABCOCK

   Clue: a 600m/1969ft hill above the Irish Sea (5,5)

Europe

23 Europe: Hitting the High Spots

Match each mountain in List 1 with the country in List 2 of which it is the highest mountain.

List 1

1. Botrange (694m/2277ft)
2. Carrantuohil (1038m/3405ft)
3. Gerlach (2655m/8711ft)
4. Grossglockner (3798m/12,461ft)
5. Kékes (1014m/3327ft)
6. Knieff (560m/1837ft)
7. Moldoveaunu (2544m/8346ft)
8. Møllehøj (107m/353ft)
9. Mulhacen (3478m/11,411ft)
10. Rysy (2503m/8212ft)
11. Vaalserberg (322m/1058ft)
12. Zugspitze (2962m/9718ft)

List 2

a. Austria
b. Belgium
c. Denmark
d. Germany
e. Hungary
f. Ireland
g. Luxembourg
h. Netherlands
i. Poland
j. Romania
k. Slovakia
l. Spain

24   European Mountain Ranges

Name the following European mountain ranges.

1. The second of Western Europe's great mountain ranges after the
    Alps, stretching from sea to ocean and containing more than
    50 peaks over 3000m/10,000ft high.

2. Literally the 'Home of the Giants', the mountain range that
    contains Norway's highest peaks.

3. The 100ml/160km-long mountain range that is the most
    extensive in Greece. Highest peak: Mount Smolikas
    (2637m/8651ft).

    (a)   Lefka Ori (White Mountains of Crete)
    (b)   PIndus
    (c)   Rhodope

4. The compact range of rocky limestone peaks in northern Spain,
    popular with climbers and cavers as well as hikers. Highest
    peak: Torre de Cerredo (2648m/8688ft).

5. The range of jagged peaks on the Polish-Slovak border that is
    the highest mountain group in the Carpathians.

6. The range of mountains that separates the Rhine and the Rhone
    on the border of France and Switzerland.

    (a)   Cévennes
    (b)   Jura
    (c)   Vosges

7. The 600ml/1000km-long mountain range that forms the spine
    of Italy. Highest peak: Corno Grande (2912m/9554ft).

8. The 50ml/80km-long Spanish mountain range that is the closest
    to Madrid. Highest peak: Pico de Panelara (2428m/7966ft).

    (a)   Sierra de Gredos
    (b)   Sierra de Guadarrama
    (c)   Sierra Nevada

9. The Mediterranean island range of which Punta la Marmora (1834m/6017ft) in the highest point on the island.

   (a) Gennargentu Massif, Sardinia
   (b) Monte CInto Massif, Corsica
   (c) Serra de Tramuntana, Majorca

10. The range of forested hills in which the Battle of the Bulge was fought, when Hitler launched one last surprise attack on the Allied advance in December 1944. High point: Haut Fagnes (694m/2277ft).

25 Ireland and Northern Ireland

1. What is the highest mountain in Ireland?

2. In which range does this mountain stand?

    (a)   Macgillicuddy's Reeks
    (b)   The Galtee Mountains
    (c)   The Slieve Mish Mountains

3. Using a separation measure of 15m/50ft of prominence
    (of summit above surroundings), how many 'Irish Munros'
    (with a height of 914m/3000ft or over) are there?

    (a)   7
    (b)   14
    (c)   21

4. What is the highest mountain in Northern Ireland?

5. What colour is the 832m/2729ft mountain that lies between the
    Lakes of Killarney and the Gap of Dunloe?

    (a)   Blue
    (b)   Green
    (c)   Purple

6. What is the Mourne Wall?

7. Which Irish mountain range constitutes the largest block of
    granite mountains in the British Isles?

    (a)   The Mourne Mountains
    (b)   The Slieve Mish Mountains
    (c)   The Wicklow Mountains

8. Where in Ireland do the third highest sea cliffs in Western
    Europe rise 688m/2257ft from the sea?

    (a)   Croaghaun, Achill Island
    (b)   Moher, County Clare
    (c)   Slieve League, County Donegal

9. Which 764m/2507ft hill is the most climbed in Ireland? On the last Sunday in July every year, more than 15,000 people make a pilgrimage to the chapel at the summit.

   (a) Arderin, Counties Laois & Offaly
   (b) Croagh Patrick, County Mayo
   (c) Errigal, County Donegal

10. Which of the three hills in Question 9 is the highest point in the Slieve Bloom Mountains? Despite a height of only 527m/1729ft, until the 17th century it was thought to be the highest in the country. It's Irish name means 'Ireland's Height'.

26 The European Alps

1. What is an alp?

2. In the 'official' list of Alpine peaks listed by the Union
    Internationale des Associations d'Alpinisme in 1994, how
    many are 4000'ers (individual mountains 4000m/13,123ft high
    or over)?

    (a) 62
    (b) 82
    (c) 102

3. Which country has the most 4000'ers?

    (a) France
    (b) Italy
    (c) Switzerland

4. When did mountain guide Jacques Balmat and doctor Michel
    Paccard make the first ascent of Mont Blanc (4810m/15,781ft),
    the highest mountain in the Alps?

    (a) 1736
    (b) 1786
    (c) 1836

5. How was a successful ascent of Mont Blanc celebrated in the
    village of Chamonix at its foot in the 19th Century?

    (a) By a dance in the main square
    (b) By the firing of cannons
    (c) By the public reading of a congratulatory letter from
         Louis XVIII

6. When was the Golden Age of Alpinism, when nearly all the
    highest peaks were climbed for the first time?

    (a) 1834–1845
    (b) 1854–1865
    (c) 1874–1885

7. There are four distinct ridges that climb to the summit of the Matterhorn. Which of the following is NOT one of these ridges?

   (a) Furggen (SE Ridge)
   (b) Italian (SW Ridge)
   (c) Mittellegi (NE Ridge)
   (d) Zmutt (NW Ridge)

8. Name one of the three peaks on which a railway climbs to the highest railway station in Europe (3454m/11,332ft).

9. To which peak does the highest cable car in Europe climb even higher than the highest railway station?

10. What is the Haute Route?

The World

27 High Country

The answer to each of the following questions is the name of a country.

1. Which country contains most of the 14 individually recognised 8000m peaks?

   (a) India
   (b) Nepal
   (c) Pakistan

2. First ascents of the Himalayan 8000m peaks were made by mountaineers from Austria, China, France, Germany, Italy, Japan, Switzerland, UK and USA. Which country produced most first ascents (i.e. three)?

3. Which country has no 4000m peaks but whose 3000m peaks include Glacier Peak, Mount Vancouver and Mount Aspiring?

4. Which of the following three African countries does NOT have its name incorporated into the name of its highest mountain?

   (a) Burundi
   (b) Cameroon
   (c) Kenya

5. Name the European country whose highest point (excluding dependent territories, autonomous overseas regions etc.) lies on an island.

6. Name the only landlocked country through which the Andes pass.

   (a) Bolivia
   (b) Colombia
   (c) Ecuador

7. Which European principality has no land lower than 840m/2756ft?

8. Ice-capped mountains occur near the equator in three places. The Andes and East Africa are two of these places. Where is the third?

9. Name the European country whose highest point for much of the 20th Century is no longer the highest point.

   (a)   Iceland
   (b)   Norway
   (c)   Sweden

10. Where does the British Empire mountain range stand beside the United States mountain range?

    (a)   Antarctica
    (b)   Australia
    (c)   Canada

28 Mountains of the World

Name the following mountains of the world.

1. A 3776m/12,388ft volcano that is perhaps the most climbed high mountain in the world. As many as 300,000 tourists, climbers and Buddhist pilgrims make the ascent every year.

2. An African volcano named for its snowcap. Its Swahili name means 'the mountain that glitters'.

3. A twin-peaked 5947m/19,512ft mountain in the Peruvian Andes that is famed for its fluted ice buttresses. The 1966 World Conference on Scenic Beauty declared it to be 'the most beautiful mountain in the world'.

4. The only major Canadian Rocky Mountain that is named after one of Canada's ten provinces. It is 3619m/11,873ft high and was first climbed in 1925 by a team from Japan.

   (a) Mount Alberta
   (b) Mount Saskatchewan
   (c) Mount Yukon

5. A 4892m/16,050ft mountain, lying in the Sentinel Range of the Ellsworth Mountains, that is the highest in Antarctica.

6. A 2917m/9570ft mountain that is the highest in its country. Its summit is called Mytikas (The Point) and one of its subsidiary tops is known as the Throne of Zeus.

7. A 6768m/22,205ft Peruvian mountain that became infamous in 1970 when an earthquake-triggered landslide on its slopes killed all 15 members of a Czech climbing expedition and buried the town of Yungay, along with most of its 20,000 inhabitants.

   (a) Huascaran
   (b) Pumasillo
   (c) Yerupaja

8. A 1084m/3556ft coastal mountain that is the home of South African rock climbing. It was first climbed in 1503 by the Portuguese admiral Antonio da Saldanha in order to determine his whereabouts.

9. A 7134m/23,406ft mountain in the Pamirs that is perhaps the easiest and most climbed 7000'er in the world, with hundreds of ascents every year.

10. A 7816m/25,644ft mountain that until 1808 was thought to be the highest mountain in the world. In 1936 it became the first 25,000ft summit ever to be climbed, by Noel Odell and Bill Tilman. After admiring the peak's beauty as a young man, American mountaineer Willi Unsoeld named his daughter after it. Tragically, she died near its summit on her father's 1976 expedition.

    (a)   Ama Dablam
    (b)   Gauri Sankar
    (c)   Nanda Devi

29 Mountain Ranges of the World

Name the following mountain ranges of the world.

1. The 4700ml/7600km-long mountain range that is the longest on earth.

2. The 250ml/400km-long mountain range whose name is Turkish for 'Black Rubble'. It lies parallel to the main crest of the Himalayas at its western end and contains some of the world's highest mountains, including 8000m peaks such as Broad Peak and Gasherbrum.

    (a)   Hindu Kush
    (b)   Karakoram
    (c)   Pamirs

3. The most northerly mountain range in Africa, with a heavy winter snow cover at the edge of the Sahara Desert. Highest peak: Toubkal (4167m/13,671ft).

4. The heavily glaciated mountain range on the Pacific coast of British Columbia, containing the highest mountain in Canada (Mount Logan, 5959m/19,551ft).

    (a)   Bugaboos
    (b)   Coast Range
    (c)   Purcell Mountains

5. The mountain range that stretches for nearly 600ml/1000km between the Black Sea and the Caspian Sea. Highest peak: Elbrus (5642m/18,511ft).

6. Literally the 'Snow Hills', the African mountain range that is better known as the 'Mountains of the Moon'. Their present name was given to them by the explorer and journalist H. M. Stanley, after whom the highest group of tops is named Mount Stanley (5109m/16,762ft).

    (a)   Drakensberg
    (b)   Ruwenzori
    (c)   Virunga

7. The major mountain system of Mexico, extending 1500ml/ 2500km southwards from the US border. Its three parts enclose the Mexican plain on the west, east and south and are consequently named Occidental, Oriental and del Sur.

   (a) Sierra Madre
   (b) Sierra Maestra
   (c) Sierra Nevada

8. The bleak mountain range around the headwaters of the River Oxus, containing the highest mountain (7495m/24,591ft) in the former Soviet Union. The range's name refers to the valleys that separate individual mountain groups.

   (a) Pindus
   (b) Pamirs
   (c) Urals

9. The highest and most extensive mountain range in Australia, bordering the Pacific Ocean for c.2170ml/3500km.

   (a) Blue Mountains
   (b) Coast Range
   (c) Great Dividing Range

10. The Turkish mountain range that forms a high barrier between the central Anatolian plain and the Mediterranean Sea. Highest peak: Demirkazik (3756m/12,323ft).

    (a) Cilo-Sat
    (b) Kackar
    (c) Taurus

30 Alps of the World

Match each Alpine mountain range in List 1 with the country in List 2 in which it can be found.

List 1

1. Alpes Montes
2. Bavarian Alps
3. Bernese Alps
4. Chuya Alps
5. Julian Alps
6. Kita Alps
7. Maritime Alps
8. Southern Alps
9. Staunings Alps
10. Stubai Alps
11. Transylvanian Alps
12. Trinity Alps

List 2

a. Austria
b. France
c. Germany
d. Greenland
e. Japan
f. New Zealand
g. Romania
h. Siberia (Russia)
i. Slovenia
j. Switzerland
k. The moon
l. USA

31 The USA

1. Of the 20 highest mountains in the USA, how many are in Alaska?

   (a)   7
   (b)   17
   (c)   27

2. Of the USA's 50 states, which has the highest average elevation (*c.*2070m/6800ft)?

   (a)   Alaska
   (b)   Colorado
   (c)   Montana

3. Which state has the most 'fourteeners' (individual mountains with a height of 4270m/14,000ft or over)?

   (a)   Alaska
   (b)   Colorado
   (c)   Montana

4. Name the famous long distance trail that runs for over 2000ml/3200km from Mount Katahdin, Maine, to Springer Mountain, Georgia.

5. Mount Everest (8848m/29,029ft), the highest mountain in the world, rises *c.*3500m/11,500ft above its southside base camp. The highest mountain in the USA, known nationally as Mount McKinley and in Alaska as Denali (6194m/20,320ft), has the highest rise above its surrounding elevations of any mountain on the surface of the earth. How high?

   (a)   *c.*3900m/13,000ft
   (b)   *c.*4700m/15,500ft
   (c)   *c.*5500m/18,000ft

6. What natural feature did President Theodore Roosevelt say was the 'one great sight every American should see'?

   (a) Grand Canyon
   (b) Yellowstone
   (c) Yosemite

7. For which of the locations in Question 6 was the world's first national park established in 1872?

8. Mount Whitney (4421m/14,505ft) is the highest mountain in the continental USA (excluding Alaska and Hawaii). Which is the second highest mountain?

   (a) Mount Elbert (Colorado)
   (b) Mount Rainier (Washington)
   (c) Mount Shasta (California)

9. Which state has the lowest high point (105m/345ft)?

   (a) Delaware
   (b) Florida
   (c) Louisiana

10. Name the Californian mountain range that John Muir dubbed 'The Range of Light'.

32 The Numbers Game

Fill in the missing numbers. Each number is greater than the number in the preceding question.

1. The Empty ____
    Clue: Arabian Peninsula sand desert.

2. ____ Gully
    Clue: a major gully at the extreme left (east) of the north face of Ben Nevis, whose first winter ascent in 1957 was hailed as a breakthrough in Scottish ice climbing.

3. ____ Dome
    Clue: a landmark summit at the head of Yosemite Valley, California, USA.

4. ____ Tier Buttress
    Clue: a Cheedale climbers' crag.

5. The ____ Sisters
    Clue: mountain spurs in Glen Coe or glacier-covered 3000m/ 10,000ft volcanoes in Oregon, USA.

6. The ____ Sisters
    Clue: a West Highland ridge containing three Munros.

7. The ____ Sisters
    Clue: sea cliffs on the south coast of England.

8. The ____ Bens
    Clue: hills in Connemara, Ireland.

9. ____ Years on Ben Nevis
    Clue: the title of W.T. Kilgour's 1905 book on the Ben Nevis observatory. The number is divisible by ten.

10. Le Massif du Mont Blanc: Les Plus Belles ____ Courses

Clue: Gaston Rébuffat's classic 1973 book on the finest routes in the Mont Blanc range. The number is divisible by ten.

11. The Valley of ____ Falls
Clue: a picturesque valley on the flanks of Mount Robson in the Canadian Rockies, fed by meltwater from hanging glaciers.

(a)   200
(b)   500
(c)   1000

12. The Valley of the ____ Smokes

Clue: a volcanic region in Katmai National Park, Alaska.

(a)   2000
(b)   5000
(c)   10,000

Specialist Subjects

33 Long Distance Trails of England and Wales

Name the following long distance trails of England and Wales.

1. Britain's longest waymarked trail, a 630ml/1013km coastal route consisting of four trails that were linked together as a continuous right of way in 1978.

   (a) South Coast Path
   (b) South East Coast Path
   (c) South West Coast Path

2. The unofficial but popular 40ml/64km trail that crosses the wildest parts of the North Yorkshire Moors and is named after an old Yorkshire funeral dirge.

3. The 56ml/90km trail that runs from Cromer to Great Yarmouth in East Anglia.

   (a) The Norfolk Coast Way
   (b) The Norfolk Broads Way
   (c) The Weavers Way

4. The 177ml/284km trail along the English-Welsh border that is named after an 8th century king of Mercia.

   (a) Alfred the Great Way
   (b) Glendower Way
   (c) Offa's Dyke Path

5. Britain's first national long distance trail, a 268ml/431km north-south trail that was finally opened in 1965 after a 30-year struggle.

6. The 53ml/85km trail around a Yorkshire city.

    (a)   Leeds Country Walk
    (b)   Sheffield Country Walk
    (c)   York Country Walk

7. The 186ml/299km trail that follows the coast of Britain's only coastal national park.

8. The 147ml/236km trail, named after former invaders, that heads south from the Humber Bridge through Lincolnshire.

    (a)   The Norman Way
    (b)   The Saxon Way
    (c)   The Viking Way

9. Which two moors does the 102ml/164km Two Moors Way link?

10. Which of the following four major rivers does NOT have a long distance trail along its valley?

    (a)   The Avon
    (b)   The Severn
    (c)   The Thames
    (d)   The Trent

34 Camping

1. What kind of tent is a geodesic tent?

2. How does a flysheet increase the warmth of a tent?

3. When using an inner tent with a flysheet, the inner tent is usually attached to the tent frame and the flysheet is draped over it. This produces maximum internal volume and allows the inner tent to be used without a flysheet if required. Some tent frames, however, are attached to the flysheet and the inner is hung from them. What advantage does this have?

4. Which is warmest on a winter's night and why?

   (a) A dark-coloured tent
   (b) A light-coloured tent
   (c) A mesh tent

5. What type of tent is a dunnel?

6. If using a groundsheet that is not attached to the tent, should it have a smaller surface area (footprint) than that of the tent or should it be larger and extend under the tent sides, and why?

7. Does a sleeping bag increase the warmth of its occupant and, if so, how?

8. On a cold night, which is the warmest place to camp and why?

   (a) In a depression
   (b) On a hillside
   (c) On a hill top

9. When camping in winter, should snowmelt for drinking be collected at night or in the morning, and why?

10. In the 1970s, in the USA, Jack Stephenson produced tents that could be used without sleeping bags. What was the principle behind them?

(a) The tent wall consisted of a waterproof exterior bonded to a fleece interior.

(b) The tent wall was double-layered and enclosed so that it could be inflated by blowing (warm) air into it.

(c) The tent wall was made from multiple layers of fabric.

35 British Mountain Ridges

Match each ridge in List 1 with the British mountain in List 2 on which it is found.

List 1

1. Bristly Ridge
2. Curved Ridge
3. Devil's Ridge
4. Fiacaill Ridge
5. Forcan Ridge
6. Lancet Edge
7. Long Leachas
8. Pinnacle Ridge (Wales)
9. Sentries' Ridge
10. Sharp Edge
11. Steel Edge
12. Tower Ridge

List 2

a. Ben Alder (Central Highlands)
b. Ben Nevis (Central Highlands)
c. Blencathra or The Saddleback (Lake District)
d. Buachaille Etive Mor (Glen Coe)
e. Cairn Lochan (Cairngorms)
f. Crib Goch (Snowdonia)
g. Glyder Fach (Snowdonia)
h. Mynnyd Mawr (Snowdonia)
i. Sgor Iutharn (Central Highlands)
j. Sgurr a' Mhaim (Central Highlands)
k. The Saddle (Western Highlands)
l. Wetherlam (Lake District)

36 Famous British Mountaineers

Name the following famous British mountaineers.

1. A mountaineer and writer whose epic crawl back to base camp following a near-fatal accident in the Peruvian Andes became the subject of the 1998 book and 2003 film *Touching the Void*.

2. A Scottish doctor who revolutionised post-war winter climbing in Scotland and who was on the first ascent of Rakaposhi (7788m/25,551ft) in 1958. He was killed while abseiling from a Scottish sea stack in 1970.

3. A leading 19th century mountaineer who made many first ascents in the Alps, the Andes and the Canadian Rockies, including the Matterhorn (Switzerland). His Alpine climbs formed the subject of his classic book *Scrambles Amongst the Alps in the Years 1860-'69*.

4. A mountaineer, explorer and travel writer who led the British Everest expedition in 1938 and disappeared while sailing across the Atlantic in 1977.

5. An English plumber who made a series of brilliant rock climbs in the early 50s and who was on the first ascent of Kangchenjunga (8586m/28,169ft) in 1955. His autobiography *The Hard Years* was published in 1967.

6. A mountaineer who was perhaps the foremost Alpinist of his generation. His classic book *My Climbs in the Alps and Caucasus* appeared in the same year in which he disappeared in an avalanche while attempting Nanga Parbat (8126m/26,660ft) in 1895.

7. An ex-army officer who made the first British ascent of the North Face of the Eiger in 1962 and led many Himalayan expeditions, including the first ascent of the South Face of Annapurna in 1970. In 1985 he reached the summit of Mount Everest at the age of 50.

8. A poet and president of the Alpine Club from 1941-44 who reached the summit of the Matterhorn (Switzerland) with an artificial limb after losing his left leg during the First World War.

9. A pioneer Victorian rock climber and Alpinist who became renowned as the 'Father of Norwegian Mountaineering' after his book *Norway: The Northern Playground* was published in 1904.

10. An English mountaineer who in 1984 became the first woman to climb an 8000m peak (Broad Peak, 8051m/26,414ft). She died in her tent near the summit of K2 (8611m/28,251ft) in 1986.

37 It's Cold Outside

1. Why are toes and fingers the first parts of the body to succumb to frostbite in cold weather?

2. Why is it important to wear a head covering in cold weather?

3. What is (i) the best and (ii) the next best insulation from the cold?

    (a) A still gas
    (b) A vacuum
    (c) Lead

4. Why are loose clothes warmer than tight clothes?

5. If, while hiking, you were to fall into a lake whose water was at freezing point, how long would you survive?
    (a) 0–0.5 minute
    (b) 0.5–3 minutes
    (c) 3–5 minutes

6. Which is warmer and why: gloves or mittens?

7. What is snow sintering?

    (a) The process by which snow crystals bond together
    (b) The process by which snowflakes form in the air
    (c) The process by which wind slab avalanches occur

8. Why should you not drink alcohol when you are cold?

9. Which insulating material has the most warmth?

    (a) Down
    (b) Fleece
    (c) Hollow fibre

10. Why is it colder in winter than summer?

38 Glaciers

1. A glacier that covers more than 50,000 sq km (19,300 sq ml) is known as an ice sheet. There are only two in the world. One is in Antarctica. Where is the other?

2. What causes a fissure in the surface of a glacier known as a crevasse?

3. With a length of c.76ml/122km, which is the longest single glacier in the northern hemisphere?

   (a) The Athabasca Glacier, Alberta, Canada
   (b) The Baltoro Glacier, Pakistan
   (c) The Hubbard Glacier, Alaska, USA

4. What is a *dry* glacier and why is it less dangerous to walk on?

5. Where on a glacier would you find a *bergschrund*?

6. What is a glacier table?

   (a) A comparative list of glaciers per country
   (b) A level, crevasse-free stretch of glacier
   (c) A rock lying on top of a column of ice

7. How would mountaineers use an ice bollard?

8. The fastest moving major glacier in the world is the Jakobshavn Glacier in Greenland. What is its approximate average rate of flow per day?
   (a) 20cm/8in
   (b) 2m/6.5ft
   (c) 20m/65ft

9. What is a nunatak?

10. What does the International Ice Patrol monitor?

   (a) The extent of the Antarctic ice sheet
   (b) The thickness of the Arctic ice cap
   (c) Iceberg movement in the North Atlantic

39 Mountain Weather

1. What is a rain shadow and what causes it?

2. The Beaufort scale of wind force runs from 0 (calm) to 11
   (violent storm: 64–73mph/103–117kph), with hurricanes rated
   12–17. What wind force is sufficient to impede progress when
   hiking?

   (a) 6
   (b) 8
   (c) 10

3. *Katabatic* winds are common in mountainous areas. What are
   they?

4. Excluding tornadoes, the highest surface wind speed ever
   recorded was 231mph/372kph on an American mountain.
   Which mountain?

   (a) Mount Baker, Washington
   (b) Mount Rainier, Washington
   (c) Mount Washington, New Hampshire

5. Which American mountain, one of the three in Question 4,
   holds the world record for the most amount of snow fallen
   during a year (28,550mm/1224ins – almost 96ft)?

6. By approximately how much does temperature decrease per
   300m/1000ft of altitude on a sunny day?

   (a) 1°C/1.8°F
   (b) 2°C/3.6°F
   (c) 3°C/5.4°F

7. When can you see your own glory?

8. In the same weather conditions, what other geographical factor affects the temperature on a mountain apart from altitude?

   (a) Latitude
   (b) Longitude
   (c) Proximity to the sea

9. Why does a cloud cap on a mountain appear stationary even in a strong wind?

10. Wind makes temperatures seem colder than they are – a phenomenon known as wind-chill. What is the effective temperature given an air temperature of 0°C/32°F and a wind speed of 40mph/64kph?

    (a) -3°C/26.6°F
    (b) -6°C/21.2°F
    (c) -9°C/15.8°F

40 Mountain Flora and Fauna

1. Which animal causes more injuries than any other to the world's hikers?

2. In which mountainous area is found Britain's only herd of wild reindeer?

   (a)   The Cairngorms
   (b)   The Paps of Jura
   (c)   Wester Ross

3. In which mountainous area, one of the three in Question 2, is found Britain's highest natural treeline?

4. Why do the north and south facing slopes of a mountain support different flora?

5. Which exterminated species was re-introduced to the Isle of Rum between 1975 and 1985?

   (a)   Bear
   (b)   White-tailed Eagle
   (c)   Wolf

6. Name Britain's only native poisonous snake.

7. What creatures, previously thought legendary, were discovered on the Muir Glacier in Alaska in 1887?

   (a)   Ice worms
   (b)   Sasquatch (Bigfoot)
   (c)   Snow leopards

8. Why do many high mountain plants have waxy leaves?

9. What is the highest confirmed altitude ever reached by a bird in flight?

   (a)   17,000ft (5181m)
   (b)   27,000ft (8229m)
   (c)   37,000ft (11,277m)

10. Which flower appears on the badge of the Austrian Alpine Club?

41 Literary Connections

1. Which mountain appears in the title of, and provides the backdrop to, a 1938 Ernest Hemingway short story that was made into a 1952 film starring Gregory Peck?

   (a) Kilimanjaro, Tanzania
   (b) Mount McKinley (Denali), Alaska, USA
   (c) The Matterhorn, Switzerland

2. Name the fictional illusory peak that gives Thomas Mann's 1924 Nobel Prize winning novel its symbolic title.

   (a) Mount Improbable
   (b) The Magic Mountain
   (c) The Mirage

3. Name the world's oldest mountaineering journal, which was founded in 1863 and is still published annually.

   (a) The Alpine Journal
   (b) The Cairngorm Club Journal
   (c) The Scottish Mountaineering Club Journal

4. In *The Dharma Bums* Jack Kerouac describes a beatnik ascent of a mountain in Yosemite National Park, California. Which mountain?

   (a) El Capitan
   (b) Half Dome
   (c) The Matterhorn

5. Which flat-topped, cliff-encircled 2810m/9219ft Venezuelan mountain inspired Sir Arthur Conan Doyle to write *The Lost World*?

   (a) Cristobal Colon
   (b) Simon Bolivar
   (c) Roraima

6. Who was the subject of James Ramsay Ullman's 1965 biography, entitled *Man of Everest* in the UK?

7. Name the fictional 12,200m/40,000ft Himalayan mountain that is climbed accidentally by the expedition porters in W. E. Bowman's classic 1956 parody of expedition books.

   (a) KO
   (b) Neverest
   (c) Rum Doodle

8. According to Felice Benuzzi's 1952 book, the ascent of which mountain was no picnic for him and his fellow Italians when they escaped from a Second World War prisoner of war camp in North Africa in order to do some climbing?

   (a) Jebel Toubkal
   (b) Kilimanjaro
   (c) Mount Kenya

9. Which poet, who invented the roundel verse form, made the first ascent of Bla Bheinn, a 928m/3044ft Munro on Skye, in 1857?

   (a) Lord Byron
   (b) Percy Bysshe Shelley
   (c) John Keats
   (d) Algernon Swinburne

10. Which poet, one of the four in Question 9 and a leading figure in the Romantic movement of the nineteenth century, climbed Lochnagar, a 1155m/3436ft Munro in the Cairngorms, at the age of 15 in 1803?

42 Films

1. In which 1975 film does Clint Eastwood climb an Alpine north face in order to catch a spy?

2. On the face of which American mountain is Cary Grant pursued by Martin Landau in Alfred Hitchcock's 1959 comedy-thriller *North by Northwest*?

3. Which mountain do Chris O'Donnell and Robin Tunney fail to climb in the 2000 film *Vertical Limit*?

   (a)   Mount McKinley (Denali), Alaska, USA
   (b)   Everest, Nepal
   (c)   K2, Pakistan

4. *Alive* tells the true story of a 1972 plane crash in the mountains and the epic walk out to civilisation that saved the survivors. In which mountain range did the plane crash?

5. How does Sean Connery's Alpine guide meet his end in the 1983 film *Five Days One Summer*?

   (a)   He falls into a crevasse
   (b)   He is killed by rockfall
   (c)   He sacrifices himself by cutting the rope

6. In which 1975 Australian film does a group of schoolgirls disappear on a rock outcrop during a Valentine's Day picnic in 1900?

7. In which 1993 film does mountain rescue ranger Sylvester Stallone have to employ all his climbing skills to fight a bunch of ruthless crooks in the Rocky Mountains?

8. Which Mediterranean volcano is the title of a 1949 film starring Ingrid Bergman?

   (a)   Etna
   (b)   Stromboli
   (c)   Vesuvius

9. Which 2000 sequel opens with Tom Cruise solo rock climbing in Utah?

10. Name the mountain range in which Humphrey Bogart and his partners search for gold in an Oscar-winning 1948 film.

11. Relaxing between space missions, Captain Kirk goes solo rock climbing on earth in *Star Trek V* (1989). On which American peak is he climbing when he falls and has to be rescued by Mr Spock in anti-gravity boots?

    (a)   Devil's Tower, Wyoming
    (b)   El Capitan, California
    (c)   Half Dome, California

12. Name the 1977 James Bond film that opened with stuntman Rick Sylvester (as James Bond) BASE jumping off the flat summit of Mount Asgard on Baffin Island with a Union Jack parachute?

Pot Pourri

43 Pot Pourri 1

1. Which Grand National winner was named after a Munro?

2. Approximately how much of the earth's 56 million sq ml (145 million sq km) land mass is above 900m/3000ft?

   (a) 5%
   (b) 15%
   (c) 25%

3. What and where is the highest restaurant/snack bar in Britain?

4. When were women admitted to the Alpine Club?

   (a) 1946
   (b) 1974
   (c) 2002

5. What unusual items of equipment were employed on the first ascent of the rock climb Great White Fright on Dover's chalk cliffs?

6. The highest sea stack in the world is Ball's Pyramid (560m/1840ft). Where is it?

   (a) Off the coast of Australia
   (b) Off the coast of Chile
   (c) Off the coast of India

7. The third ascent of Ball's Pyramid was made by a French team in 1985. Why was it the last?

8. What is the height of the South Pole?

   (a) 0m/0ft
   (b) 63m/211ft
   (c) 2801m/9186ft

9. Mountain bikers were first allowed to compete in the 22ml/35km Man v Horse Marathon over the hills around Llanwrtyd Wells in 1985. In which decade, if any, did the first mountain biker win?

10. Where is the nearest mountain to Britain on which you can join the mile-high club? (One mile = 5280ft/1609m)

   (a)   Ardennes, Belgium
   (b)   Jura, France
   (c)   Massif Central, France

44 Pot Pourri 2

1. The Ordnance Survey was founded in 1791. Why is it so called?

2. Where is Ben Lomond National Park?

   (a)   British Columbia, Canada
   (b)   Scotland
   (c)   Tasmania, Australia

3. What would you be doing if indulging in *langlauf*?

4. When Sir John Hunt, leader of the first successful Everest expedition in 1953, was asked in 1985 to write an article on his favourite mountain, which surprising Lake District hill did he choose?

   (a)   Castlerigg Fell, east of Derwent Water
   (b)   Crag Hill, west of Derwent Water
   (c)   Latrigg, north of Derwent Water

5. What is it forbidden to wear in an Alpine climbers' hut?

6. In 1953, the year that Mount Everest was first climbed, the highest known seamount (submarine mountain) was discovered between Samoa and New Zealand. How high does it rise above the ocean bed?

   (a)   4650m/15,500ft
   (b)   8700m/28,500ft
   (c)   11,100m/36,500ft

7. What is a Tyrolean Traverse?

8. Where do the Berkshire Hills separate Northampton from Sheffield?

   (a)   Berkshire, England
   (b)   Massachusetts, USA
   (c)   Tasmania, Australia

9. In which language did the word 'anorak' originate?

10. On the 1962 joint British-Russian Pamirs expedition, Russian climbers were unsure how to address expedition leader Sir John Hunt. What did their colleague, Manchester climber Joe Brown, advise them was the correct form of address?

   (a) 'Balls to you, Sir John'
   (b) 'Screw you, Sir John'
   (c) 'Up yours, Sir John'

45 Pot Pourri 3

1. Which country's national park has the highest average elevation of any national park in the world?

2. According to mountaineer and writer Showell Styles in 1958, how much should a good pair of walking boots cost?

   (a) £6
   (b) £12
   (c) £18

3. The ancient Greek philosopher Empedocles made one of the first recorded ascents of a mountain when he committed suicide at the summit. How?

4. Of which pinnacle was there a mass ascent on 28 June 1986, to commemorate the centenary of the first ascent?

   (a) Inaccessible Pinnacle, Skye
   (b) Napes Needle, Lake District
   (c) Fisher Tower, Utah, USA

5. Mount Everest was first definitely climbed in 1953. In which decade did the first woman reach the summit?

6. To the winner of which annual mountain race is the MacFarlane Trophy awarded?

   (a) The Ben Nevis race
   (b) The Cairn Gorm race
   (c) The Lochnagar race

7. When tying ropes together, under which circumstances would a double sheet bend be used?

8. King Albert 1 of the Belgians was a keen Alpinist. What caused his death in the Ardennes in 1934?

   (a) An abseiling accident
   (b) An avalanche
   (c) A rockfall

9. Where did modern avalanche control begin?

   (a) Dolomites, Italy
   (b) Ruapehu, New Zealand
   (c) Whistler, Canada

10. What is the world governing body of mountaineering called?

46   Pot Pourri 4

1. With what did George Leigh Mallory fill his pockets, for sustenance, when climbing Mount Everest?

2. The Karrimor International Mountain Marathon (KIMM), known as the Original Mountain Marathon since 2010, was one of the first mountain adventure races. It is a two-day event held in a different area of the UK every year. When was it first held?

   (a)   1948
   (b)   1968
   (c)   1988

3. What does Triple Divide Mountain in Glacier National Park, Montana, USA, divide?

4. In which year was the little known 3482m/11,424ft summit of Thabana Ntlenyana (meaning Beautiful Little Mountain) in Lesotho discovered to be the highest mountain in Africa south of Kilimanjaro?

   (a)   1951
   (b)   1971
   (c)   1991

5. How did Voltaire explain the presence of sea shells on mountain tops?

6. What is the real reason for the presence of sea shells on mountain tops?

7. The pores in a Goretex membrane are c.20,000 times smaller than a drop of water. Approximately how many pores are there per square inch?

   (a)   9 million
   (b)   9 thousand million
   (c)   9 million million

8. Why did many early Alpinists object to the use of crampons?

9. Trigonometrical stations (trig points or pillars) were first placed in prominent locations in 1935 to aid resurveying of Britain by triangulation. They have been superceded by digital mapping using GPS satellites and are now disappearing from the countryside. How many were there originally?

(a) 1216
(b) 3378
(c) 6557

10. The Sea of Rains is bordered by the Jura, Alps, Caucasus, Apennine and Carpathian mountain ranges. Where is it?

(a) Europa (a moon of Jupiter)
(b) Mars
(c) The moon

47 Pot Pourri 5

1. In which language did the word 'cagoule' originate?

2. The Slickrock Trail at Moab, Utah, USA, is perhaps the world's most famous mountain biking trail, but for what kind of vehicle was it originally designed in 1969?

    (a) Jeeps
    (b) Motor cycles
    (c) Quad bikes

3. Why are some river valleys V-shaped and some U-shaped?

4. Name the grandson of King Victor Emmanuel II of Italy, whose expeditions made the first ascents of Mount St Elias in North America (5489m/18,008ft) in 1897 and Mount Stanley in the Ruwenzori of Africa (5109m/16,762ft) in 1906, and reached a height of 6250m/20,500ft on K2 in 1909.

    (a) Luigi, Duke of the Abruzzi
    (b) Ludwig, Prince of Holstein
    (c) Umberto, Count of Lombardy

5. How did Mount Cook, the highest mountain in New Zealand, lose 10m of height in 1991, reducing its elevation from 3764m/12,349ft to 3754m/12,316ft?

6. How long will it take a plastic bag dropped in the wilderness to decompose?

    (a) 1–5 years
    (b) 5–10 years
    (c) 10–20 years

7. What would you do with *Bergstiegeressen*?

8. During the 1970 Annapurna south face expedition, Don Whillans found himself alone in a high camp without food until Scot Dougal Haston reached him. What was the only food that Haston had brought with him?

   (a) Dundee fruit cake
   (b) Haggis
   (c) Porridge oats

9. Buttes and mesas are hills that have steep, often rocky, sides and flat tops. What is the difference between them?

10. Where, outside France, is Mont Blanc (3600m/11,800ft) the highest mountain in the Alps?

   (a) Europa (a moon of Jupiter)
   (b) Mars
   (c) The moon

48   Pot Pourri 6

1. The second highest mountain in the world is K2 (8611m/ 28,251ft). Of what is the 'K' in K2 an abbreviation?

2. Where is the lowest point on the land surface of the earth?

    (a)   Dead Sea, Israel
    (b)   Death Valley, California, USA
    (c)   Qattara Depression, Egypt

3. As a shelter from the elements, what is the only permanent dome that can be built without a scaffold?

4. What is measured by hypsometry?

    (a)   Height
    (b)   Mass
    (c)   Verticality

5. When photographer George Shadbolt climbed on the island of Sark in 1912, what local fauna did he famously suggest using for portable handholds?

6. Which 15th Century Italian painter climbed part-way up Monte Rosa in the Alps (4634m/15,203ft) and as a result concluded that glaciers were made from layers of hail?

    (a)   Da Vinci
    (b)   Michelangelo
    (c)   Raphael

7. In which country, with a height of c.860m/2820ft, are the highest sea cliffs in Europe?

8. In which country, with a height of c.1010m/3315ft, are the highest sea cliffs in the world?

    (a)   Chile
    (b)   New Guinea
    (c)   USA

9. Studies done on long distance backpackers on the Appalachian Trail in the eastern USA show that they always lose weight, no matter how much food they carry. Why?

10. Which lunar record, set on the Descartes Highlands in 1972, is held by US astronauts John Watts Young and Charles Duke?

    (a) High jump record
    (b) Long jump record
    (c) Surface height reached

49   Pot Pourri 7

1. Which country has the lowest highpoint in the world?

   (a)   Bahamas
   (b)   Maldives
   (c)   Seychelles

2. By what original method did Jean-Marc Boivin descend from the summit of Mount Everest in 1988?

3. When you hike into the Grand Canyon, how many years into the geological past are you stepping for every foot you descend?

   (a)   1000 years
   (b)   200,000 years
   (c)   1 million years

4. How did 'La Montagne' (The Mountain) take part in the 1789 French Revolution?

5. Owing to the fact that the earth is not a perfect sphere, the summit of the highest mountain (Mount Everest) is not the furthest point from the centre of the earth. Which mountain summit is furthest from the centre of the earth?

   (a)   Aconcagua (6960m/22,837ft, Argentina)
   (b)   Chimborazo (6268m/20,564ft, Ecuador)
   (c)   Kilimanjaro (5895m/19,341ft, Tanzania)

6. On which of the three mountains in Question 5 is the highest climbers' hut in the world?

7. The Alps are 'fold mountains', formed by the folding of the earth's crust. Where in the world are new fold mountains being formed at present?

   (a)   Off the east coast of India
   (b)   Off the west coast of South America
   (c)   Nowhere

8. Besides 'folding', there are three other ways in which mountains are built. Name two of them.

9. Which herb takes its name from the Greek for 'joy of the mountain'?

   (a)   Cardamom
   (b)   Oregano
   (c)   Tarragon

10. How are heights measured on the moon and other planets that have no sea level?

50   Pot Pourri 8

1. The world's first recorded Alpine rock climb was of Mont
    Aiguille (2085m/6841ft), a crag-fringed, flat-topped peak in
    south-east France. When did this take place?

    (a)   1492
    (b)   1666
    (c)   1812

2. Running and cycling are two of the three events in the New
    Zealand Coast to Coast multi-endurance race across the
    mountains of the South Island. What is the third event?

3. Where is the Top of the World Provincial Park?

    (a)   Canada
    (b)   India
    (c)   New Zealand

4. What is Andinismo?

5. Which provides more lasting energy?

    (a)   A jam sandwich
    (b)   Chocolate
    (c)   Nuts

6. In which century were women first allowed to climb Mount Fuji,
    Japan (3776m/12,388ft)?

7. After four unsuccessful attempts, American mountaineer and
    feminist Annie Smith Peck finally made the first ascent of
    Huascaran in the Andes in 1908. How old was she?

    (a)   22
    (b)   58
    (c)   73

8. Why is it difficult to walk in a Karman Vortex Street?

9. What are the Bungle Bungles?

10. Would you recommend this book to your friends?

Answers

1   MUNROS: GENERAL

1. The Central Highlands: 73 Munros. The Southern Highlands have 46, the Central Highlands have 46, the Cairngorms have 50, the Western Highlands have 62, the Northern Highlands have 38 and the Islands have 13.

2. Both the Central Highlands (Ben Nevis area) and the Cairngorms contain four 4000ft (1220m) Munros.

3. (a) 137.

4. Mull. Ben More.

5. (c) Geal Charn (White Cairn – all four are in the Central Highlands). N.B. Two are spelt Geal-Charn and Geal-charn. Three Munros are called Carn Dearg (Red Cairn – all in the Central Highlands), while two are called Ben More (Big Mountain – one in the Southern Highlands and one on the Isle of Mull), together with Ben More Assynt in the Northern Highlands. There are also three Munros called An Socach (The Snout – one in the Cairngorms and two in the Western Highlands).

6. A' Bhuidheanach Bheag, above the A9 at Drumochter Pass in the Cairngorms.

7. Beinn Teallach (Glen Spean, Central Highlands).

8. (b) Cairn Gorm. In the original 1891 Tables it had two Tops, but a major revision in 1921 awarded it nine.

9. (a) A. E. Robertson (1870–1958). A Church of Scotland minister, he completed his round of the Munros on Meall Dearg (Glen Coe) in 1901, but whether he actually summited on a couple of occasions is debated, and summits such as the Inaccessible Pinnacle on Skye were not regarded as Munros at the time.

10. 226. The latest (1997) published edition of Munro's Tables lists 227 Tops, including Knight's Peak, a rock pinnacle on Pinnacle Ridge of Sgurr nan Gillean, Skye. However, in September 2013, Knight's Peak was re-measured using a Global Positioning System receiver and found to have a height of only 914.24 metres (2999 feet 5½ inches). Consequently, it will be removed from the next published edition of Munro's Tables, leaving 226 Tops.

2 MUNROS: THE SOUTHERN HIGHLANDS

1. (a) Ben Lomond, c.30ml/48km north-west of Glasgow.
2. Ben Lui. The mine lies on the slopes of Beinn a' Chuirn above Cononish Farm.
3. (a) A castellated rock formation on the north ridge.
4. (a) Ben Lawers, near Loch Tay (1214m/3983ft). Further west near Crianlarich, Ben More is 1174m/3852ft and Stob Binnein is 1165m/3822ft.
5. (c) Schiehallion, now fancifully marketed to tourists as 'Fairy Hill of the Caledonians'.
6. (c) Meall nan Tarmachan when climbed from the 549m high point of the Lochan na Lairige road. Height gain, avoiding the climb over the intermediate top of Creag an Lochain: c.495m/ 1625ft. Beinn Heasgarnich height gain from the 505m high point of the Glen Lochay-Glen Lyon road: c.570m/1870ft. Meall Buidhe height gain from the 414m high point of the Loch an Daimh road: c.530m/1740ft.
7. (c) St Columba, a 6th Century Irish monk who introduced Christianity to the Picts of the country that was to become Scotland. The Irish were known to the Picts as Scotti, hence the country's modern name.
8. (a) 1 hour 5 minutes 51 seconds. The record was set by Prasad Prasad in 2010.
9. There are two Ben Vorlichs in the Southern Highlands.
10. (a) The area was once well known for its wild cats. Coincidentally, when viewed from any of the ridges that surround the corrie, the lochan's outline looks like a sitting cat.

3 MUNROS: THE CENTRAL HIGHLANDS

1. (c) Sgorr Dhonuill (NN 040555), overlooking Loch Linnhe. Beinn Sgulaird, overlooking Loch Creran, is 1.3km east (NN 053460). Ben Cruachan, overlooking Loch Etive, is 2.9km east (NN 069304).
2. (a) Deer. 'Roaring' as in 'rutting'.
3. (a) An Gearanach.
4. (b) Ben Nevis.

5. (d) Aonach Eagach. The other three mountains had satellite Tops elevated to Munro status, doubling their Munro tally from one to two. Aonach Eagach already sported two Munros.
6. Ben Cruachan.
7. (b) Beinn Sgulaird.
8. Beinn na Lap, situated in roadless country near Corrour railway station on the West Highland Railway Line.
9. (b) Am Bodach is a Top of Meall Dearg, the eastern Munro of Aonach Eagach in Glen Coe.
10. Stob. There are 16 Bens, 8 Sgurrs and 18 Stobs.

4 MUNROS: THE CAIRNGORMS

1. (c) Mount Keen (NO 409869), c.30m/48km from Stonehaven on the east coast. Morven (NJ 377040; a Corbett) is 0.3km to the west. Ben Avon (NJ 131018) is 2.7km to the west.
2. Lochnagar (1155m/3436ft), south of Balmoral.
3. (b) The Cairnwell when climbed from the 665m high point of the A93 at the Cairnwell Pass. Height gain: c.270m/885ft. Cairngorm height gain from the 620m high point of the Coire Cas road: c.450m/1475ft. A' Bhuidheanach Bheag height gain from the 425m high point of the A9 at Drumochter Pass: c.510m/1675ft.
4. Glas Tulaichean.
5. (b) Carn an t-Sagairt Mor. The wreckage is of an English Electric Canberra that crashed here in 1956.
6. Two: Sgor Gaoith and Mullach Clach a' Bhlair. In 1981 three Munros were demoted to Tops. Added to two existing Tops, this now makes Sgor Gaoith tie with two other Munros in having the most number of satellite Tops in the Tables (five).
7. (a) The Western Cairngorms Plateau between Braeriach and Sgor an Lochain Uaine. The River Dee begins on the plateau at the Wells of Dee and drops from the plateau at the Falls of Dee.
8. Beinn a' Bhuird. The Gaelic name means Table Mountain.
9. (a) Ben Macdui. In 1810 the Rev. George Keith made the first recorded ascent and took altitude measurements with his barometer, while his son did the same on Ben Nevis.
10. Ben Macdui.

5 MUNROS: THE WESTERN HIGHLANDS

1. (b) Ladhar Bheinn (NG 823039) on the Knoydart peninsula. Beinn Sgritheall (NG 835126) is 1.2km to the east. Tom na Gruagaich (NG 859601) is 3.6km to the east.
2. Sgurr na Ciche, in Knoydart.
3. (a) Carn Eighe (1183m/3881ft). Sgurr Fiona is 1060m/3477ft. Spidean a' Choire Leith is 1055m/3461ft.
4. Beinn Sgritheall above the north shore of Loch Hourn.
5. (c) Sgurr nan Ceannaichean. In 2009 re-measurement by GPS satellite gave it a height of 913.43m (2996ft). It was duly removed from Munro's Tables and added to Corbett's Tables.
6. (b) Sgurr nan Ceathreamhnan.
7. Ben Attow (Long Mountain).
8. (a) Beinn Fhionnlaidh. Unless a boat can be chartered along Loch Mullardoch to the north, the Munro is now normally climbed as an add-on return trip to the ascent of Carn Eighe from Glen Affric to the south.
9. A' Ghlas-bheinn. The height of the Falls of Glomach is often given as 113m/370ft, although this includes some lower falls below the main fall. The main fall drops c.25m/80ft to a rock buttress, then another c.66m/220ft to the lower falls. They are difficult to view and this can cause measurement discrepancies and exaggerations.
10. (c) Liathach. The other two mountains had satellite Tops elevated to Munro status, doubling their Munro tally from one to two. Liathach already sported two Munros.

6 MUNROS: THE NORTHERN HIGHLANDS

1. (a) Ben Hope, near the north coast.
2. (c) Sgurr Mor (1110m/3641ft). Beinn Dearg is 1084m/3556ft. Spidean a' Choire Leith is 1055m/3461ft.
3. (a) Beinn a' Chlaidheimh. Re-measurement by GPS satellite in 2011 gave it a height of 913.96m (2998ft) and in 2012 it was deleted from Munro's Tables and added to Corbett's Tables.
4. Ben Wyvis.
5   (b) Geological Park (Geopark), part of the European Geoparks Network.

6. (a) An Teallach. Beinn Eighe and Liathach both have two Munros and four Tops.

7. The Fannichs, named after remote, 7½ml/12km-long, Loch Fannich in Wester Ross.

8. Slioch, above Loch Maree.

9. (c) Liathach. The other two mountains had satellite Tops elevated to Munro status, doubling their Munro tally from one to two. Liathach already sported two Munros.

10. (b) Conival, near Inchnadamph.

7 MUNROS: BEN NEVIS

1. (b) Pinnacle Ridge. The fourth classic north face ridge is Observatory Ridge.

2. The CMD arête connects Ben Nevis to neighbouring Munro Carn Mor Dearg.

3. (a) Twice as much. On average there are 171ins/4350mm of rain per annum at the summit of Ben Nevis compared to 81ins/2050mm in Fort William at its foot (and 23ins/580mm in London).

4. (b) Two hours.

5. (c) Charles Inglis Clark. Built in 1928, the hut was donated to the SMC by members and mountaineers William and Jane Inglis Clark, in memory of their son Charles, who was killed in the First World War. It is affectionately known as the CIC Hut.

6. (b) 142ins/360cm.

7. (c) Because she was a woman. Women were not officially allowed to start the race at the same time as men until 1982.

8. (c) Sassenach was first climbed in 1954 by English climbers Joe Brown and Don Whillans, who named it after hearing an envious cry of 'English bastards!'

9. (c) John Muir Trust.

10. Named after Scotland's highest mountain, Ben Nevis is the colonial name of a 489m/1604ft hill in Hong Kong, which reverted from Britain to China in 1997. The Chinese name for the hill is now Hung Fa Chai.

8   MUNROS: HISTORY

1. (b) Stuchd an Lochain, Southern Highlands. Colin was more famous for abducting ladies and executing Macdonalds than Munro bagging. His ascent was made while deer stalking.

2. (b) Mount Keen, Cairngorms. Recounting his time at the summit, Taylor wrote that the cloud 'yielded so friendly a deaw, that it did moisten thorow all my clothes; when the old proverbe of a Scottish Miste was verified, in wetting me to the skinne'. No change there, then.

3. (b) To search for botanical specimens. Robertson was an Edinburgh botanist.

4. (c) To make meteorological observations. The ruins of the observatory are still a prominent summit feature.

5. (a) Coire Odhar in the Lawers Range. The hut had to be demolished in 1999 after being blown down by a storm.

6. (c) Meall a' Bhuiridh at the head of Glen Coe.

7. Ben Lawers, Loch Tay, Southern Highlands.

8. (a) To estimate the mass of the earth. Maskelyne took astronomical observations at various locations to see how much they were affected by gravitational pull. From these readings he was able to estimate the mass of the isolated mountain and extrapolate from this to the mass of the earth.

9. (c) Schiehallion. Hutton was part of Maskelyne's expedition (see Answer 8). His task was to survey the mountain. To simplify presentation of his findings, he came up with the idea of drawing lines to join points of equal height on the map.

10. (a) Carn a' Chlamain. At the summit Queen Victoria found the view 'beautiful, nothing but mountains all around us, and the solitude, the complete solitude, very impressive'.

9   MUNROS: ODD ONE OUT

1. They are all Munros that have names preceded by 'The', except *Cairn Bannoch*.

2. They are all Munros in the Cuillin of Skye, except Sgurr Mhor, which is in Torridon.

3. They are all Munros that have ski lifts on their slopes, except Glas Tulaichean.

4. They are all Munros on the Knoydart peninsula, except Lurg Mhor, which is near Glen Carron further north.

5. They are all mountains that have both a Big & Little Munros, e.g. Aonach Mor & Aonach Beag, except Monadh Mor.

6. They are all Munros on the Five Sisters ridge in Kintail, except Sgurr nan Conbhairean further east.

7. They are all Munros whose highest points require a scramble, except Gulvain.

8. They are all Munros that have a vehicle track almost to their summits, except Beinn a' Bhuird, whose south-side vehicle track was rewilded in the 1990s.

9. They are all Munros whose names are also the names of lochs, except Ben Ossian, which does not exist.

10. They are all Munros, except the Glen Shiel An Socach, which does not exist.

10 MUNROS: ANAGRAMS

1. Ben Lomond.
2. The Cairnwell.
3. Cairn Gorm.
4. Ben Lawers.
5. Ben Macdui.
6. Sgurr na Ciche.
7. Ben Chonzie.
8. The Devil's Point.
9. Ben More.
10. Ben Alder.
11. Lochnagar.
12 Schiehallion.
13. Derry Cairngorm.
14. Ben Nevis.
15. Creag Meagaidh.

11 SCOTTISH MOUNTAIN & HILL RANGES

1. The Grey Corries. Highpoint: Stob Choire Claurigh (1177m/3861ft).

2. (b) The Cairngorms (*gorm* is Gaelic for *blue*). Formerly known as the Monadh Ruadh (*ruadh* is Gaelic for *red*). Highpoint: Ben Macdui (1309m/4296ft).

3. The Black Mount. Highpoint: Creise (1100m/3609ft).

4. (b) The Hills of Cromdale or the Cromdale Hills. The traditional Scottish song *The Haughs o' Cromdale* commemorates the 1690 Battle of Cromdale on the haughs (low ground), in which government forces routed Jacobite forces.

5. The Arrochar Alps. The highest Munro is Beinn Ime (1011m/3316ft), but the most striking mountain is the rock peak (and Corbett) known as The Cobbler (884m/2901ft).

6. (b) The Ochils, north-west of Edinburgh. Highpoint: Ben Cleuch (721m/2366ft). The Campsies are north of Glasgow. The Pentlands are south of Edinburgh.

7. The Monadh Liath. Highpoint: Carn Dearg (945m/3100ft). *Liath* is Gaelic for *grey*, highlighting the difference between the range's mica schist geology and the granite landforms of the Monadh Ruadh (Cairngorms) across the Spey valley.

8. (b) The Cuillin of Skye. Highpoint: Sgurr Alasdair (992m/3255ft). There are no Munros on the islands of Jura and Rum.

9. The Mamores. Highpoint: Binnein Mor (1130m/3707ft).

10. (b) The Lowther Hills. Highpoint: Green Lowther (732m/2402ft). The two highest villages in Scotland are Leadhills and Wanlockhead in Lanarkshire. The Ladder Hills are east of Aviemore. The Moorfoot Hills are south of Edinburgh.

12 SCOTTISH CORBETTS

1. Goatfell. The other three Corbetts on Arran are Beinn Tarsuinn (826m/2710ft), Cir Mhor (799m/2621ft) and Caisteal Abhail (847m/2779ft).

2. (a) Beinn an Lochain. Ben Donich (847m/2779ft) and The Cobbler (884m/2900ft) are neighbouring Corbetts to the south.

3. (a) Clisham (now named An Cliseam in Gaelic on OS map). Oreval (662m/2172ft, Oireaval on OS map) and Ullaval (659m/2162ft, Ulabhal on OS map) are nearby hill tops.

4. (c) Foinaven. Nearby Arkle to the south (787m/2582ft) and Cranstackie to the north (800m/2624ft) are also Corbetts.

5. (c) Beinn Dearg. Baosbheinn (875m/2870ft) and Beinn an Eoin (855m/2805ft) are nearby Corbetts to the north.

6. (b) Beinn an Oir. Beinn Shiantaidh (755m/2477ft) and Beinn a' Chaolais (734m/2408ft) are the two lower Paps.

7. (b) Askival. Ainshval, the only other Corbett on Rum, is 781m/2652ft. Nearby Hallival is 722m/2368ft.

8 The Sow of Atholl.

9. Beinn Trilleachan.

10. Ben Loyal.

13 THE ISLE OF SKYE

1. (b) 12.

2. (a) Sgurr Dearg. Although a Munro in 1891, its summit was replaced as a Munro in the 1921 Tables by the adjacent Inaccessible Pinnacle (986m/3236ft), which overtops it by 8m/27ft. In 1891, Sgurr Dearg was considered to be the Munro because it was the mountain on which the pinnacle stood. Only later was the term 'Munro' applied to the highest point. In 1997, Sgurr Dearg's summit was considered to be too close to the pinnacle to remain in the Tables at all.

3. (b) Knight's Peak, a rock pinnacle on Pinnacle Ridge of Sgurr na Gillean. However, this was demoted from Munro's Tables again in 2013 (see Answer 1.10).

4. (a) Bla Bheinn, a Cuillin Munro isolated from the main ridge.

5. (a) Its renowned *gendarme* (literally 'policeman' in French). This was a rock tower that guarded the route to the upper ridge.

6. (a) 2. Garbh-bheinn (808m/2652ft) near Torrin and Glamaig (775m/2543ft) near Sligachan.

7. (a) Sgiath-bheinn an Uird (294m/965ft). Sgurr na Caorach is 280m/919ft. Sgurr na h-Iolaire is 292m/959ft.

8. (b) Healabhal Mhor and Healabhal Bheag are more commonly known as MacLeod's Tables owing to their flat-topped summits. Beinn na Boineid (Bonnet Mountain) is a hill to their south, while MacLeod's Maidens are sea stacks near Idrigill Point further south still.

9. (c) The Old Man of Storr. The 50m/165ft pinnacle was first climbed by Don Whillans in 1955.

10. (b) Spar Cave, near Elgol in the parish of Strath in South Skye. The 'spars' were stalactites, none of which now remain. Candlestick Cave is near Idrigill Point south of Dunvegan. Uamh Oir is on the north coast near Duntulm.

14 SCOTTISH ISLAND HIGHPOINTS

1. An Sgurr   (d)   Eigg
2. Askival   (k)   Rum
3. Beinn an Oir   (h)   Jura
4. Ben Hough   (l)   Tiree
5. Clisham   (e)   Harris
6. Dun Caan   (j)   Raasay
7. Dun I   (g)   Iona
8. Goat Fell   (a)   Arran
9. Heaval   (b)   Barra
10. Mealisval   (i)   Lewis
11. Ward Hill   (f)   Hoy
12. Windy Hill   (c)   Bute

15 SCOTLAND: WHAT & WHERE?

1. The Lost Valley is a colloquial name for Coire Gabhail, a secluded corrie on Bidean nam Bian in Glen Coe. The MacDonalds are reputed to have used it as a hiding place for their cattle (or anyone else's, hence its Gaelic name, meaning Corrie of the Bounty).

2. The Ring of Steall is a horseshoe of peaks above Steall waterfall in the Mamores (Glen Nevis), consisting of four Munros and three Tops. The name derives from the English mispronunciation of Steall (*Shtyowl*) as *Steel*. The Ring of Steel is a time-honoured military encircling strategy.

3. The Barns of Bynack are a group of granite tors on the south ridge of Bynack More in the Cairngorms.
4. The Executioner's Tooth (or Basteir Tooth) is a prominent rock tower west of Am Basteir, a Munro of which the Tooth is a Top in Munro's Tables. Am Basteir means The Executioner in Gaelic. In September 2014, the Tooth was re-measured using a Global Positioning System receiver and found to have a height of 917.16 metres (3009 feet), thus confirming its status in Munro's Tables.
5. The Grey Mare's Tail is an impressive 46m/175ft waterfall near Kinlochleven.
6. Lord Berkeley's Seat is a 1030m/3379ft peak in the Northern Highlands, one of several Tops on An Teallach.
7. The Tailors' Stone (Clach nan Taillear in Gaelic) is a rock in the Lairig Ghru (a major Cairngorms pass) where, according to legend, a group of tailors died in a blizzard while attempting to cross the pass for a bet.
8. The Witch's Step (Ceum na Caillich in Gaelic) is a rocky gap in the east ridge of Caisteal Abhail on the north side of Glen Sannox, Arran.
9. The Bloody Stone is a large boulder in Harta Corrie in the Cuillin of Skye. It marks the site of a clan battle between the MacDonalds and MacLeods.
10. The Colonel's Bed is a rocky recess in the gorge of the Ey Burn west of Braemar in the Cairngorms. It is named after John Farquharson of Inverey, called the 'Black Colonel' on account of his dark appearance, who hid here from government troops following defeat at the Battle of Killicrankie in 1689.
11. Argyll's Eyeglass is a colloquial name for the hole in the summit rock of The Cobbler in the Arrochar Alps (Southern Highlands).
12. The Giant's Staircase is a step-like succession of scramblers' crags on the north side of Stob Ban in the Grey Corries range (Central Highlands).
13. The Streak of Lightning is a zigzagging vehicle track that climbs Broad Cairn above Loch Muick on the south side of Lochnagar (Cairngorms).

14. Cluny's Cage is a rock shelter on the hillside above Alder Bay on Loch Ericht, where Cluny MacPherson helped 'Bonnie Prince Charlie' hide from government troops following the Jacobite defeat at the Battle of Culloden in 1746.

15. The White Lady is a piste (groomed ski run) on Cairn Gorm. Also the name of the chairlift that accessed the run prior to the building of the funicular railway.

16 CRYPTIC SCOTTISH MOUNTAINS & HILLS

1. Cairn Gorm. An anagram of 'minor crag'.
2. Goatfell.
3. Ben Lawers. Law-y-ers.
4. Driesh. Dries-h.
5. The Saddle.
6. The Cobbler. Ben Arthur is its more formal name.
7. Ben Alder. Ben-Al-der.
8. Canisp. A bit of 'DunCAN IS Plodding up'.
9. Mount Keen.
10. Slioch. 'Slioc' ('coils' back) + 'h'(ard).
11. Creise. Some of 'massaCRE IS Evident'.
12. Ben Tee. Bent (crooked) + 'ee' (the odd letters of 'even').
13. Streap. Backwards 'parts' around 'e' (the end letter of 'ridge').
14. Mayar. May (month five) + 'ar' (six months, i.e. half of 'year')
15. An Teallach. An anagram of 'all tea' and (c)'hanc'(e). Also: the name means 'The Forge' in Gaelic.

17 ENGLISH MOUNTAINS & HILLS

1. (c) Skiddaw (931m/3055ft), near Keswick in the Lake District.
2. (a) Cross Fell (893m/2930ft) in the Pennines. The Cheviot is 815m/2675ft. Great Shunner Fell is 716m/2350ft.
3. (c) The Cheviot, in the Cheviot Hills in Northumberland. Great Shunner Fell and Cross Fell are both further south in the Pennines.
4. Roseberry Topping, near Middlesbrough on the North York Moors.

5. (c) Whernside (736m/2415ft). Ingleborough is 724m/2376ft. Pen-y-ghent is 694m/2278ft.

6. (c) High Willhays (621m/2037ft), the highest point on Dartmoor, Devon. Dunkery Beacon (519m/1703ft) is the highest point on Exmoor. Brown Willy (420m/1378ft) is the highest point on Bodmin Moor.

7. (b) Beacon Hill, Norfolk. Great Wood Hill, the highest point in Suffolk, is 128m/419ft. Chrishall Common, the highest point in Essex, is 147m/482ft.

8. Kinder Scout.

9. (c) Mam Tor.

10. (b) Carn Brea, an ancient hilltop settlement near Redruth in Cornwall.

18 WELSH MOUNTAINS & HILLS

1. Fourteen, fifteen or sixteen, depending on the criteria used. Traditionally there are fourteen. Following metric re-measurement in the 1970s and 1980s, the minor rise of Garnedd Uchaf was given a height of 926m/3038ft and is now regarded by some as a fifteenth 3000'er. The castellated rock outcrop of Castell y Gwynt has a height of 975m/3198ft and is regarded by some as a sixteenth 3000'er.

2. (c) Glyder Fawr. Re-surveying raised its height from 999m/3278ft to 1000.8m/3283ft. Carnedd Daffyd and Crib y Ddysgl were already on the list of Welsh 1000m/3281ft peaks.

3. Cnicht, near Beddgelert in North Wales.

4. (a) The Arans, east of Dolgellau. Highpoint: Aran Fawddy (905m/2969ft). The highpoint of the Arenigs is Arenig Fawr (854m/2801ft). The highpoint of the Nantlle Ridge is Craig Cwm Silyn (734m/2408ft).

5. Cadair Idris (Chair of Idris), near Dolgellau in North Wales.

6. (b) Moel Siabod.

7. (b) Plynlimon Fawr, the highest point in Mid Wales.

8. Llanberis.

9. (a) Foel Cwmcerwyn (536m/1759ft). Foel Drygarn is 363m/1192ft. Foel Eryr is 468m/1536ft. All are in the Preseli Hills.

10. They slid down the line, sitting on a flat rock placed on the central rack of the line, with a foot on each outside rail for balance and braking. (Do not try this!)

19 MOUNTAIN & HILL RANGES OF ENGLAND & WALES

1. The Carneddau, North Wales. Highpoint: Carnedd Llywelyn 1064m/3491ft).
2. (c) The Mendips. Highpoint: Black Down (268m/880ft).
3. (b) The Glyders. Highpoint: Glyder Fawr (1000m/3283ft).
4. (c) The Rhinogs. Highpoint: Rhinog Fawr (720m/2363ft).
5. The Langdale Pikes. Highpoint: Harrison Stickle (736m/2415ft).
6. (a) The Chilterns. Highpoint: Haddington Hill (267m/876ft).
7. (b) The Cotswolds. Highpoint: Cleeve Hill (330m/1083ft).
8. The Arans. Highpoint: Aran Fawddwy (905m/2969ft).
9. The Malverns. Highpoint: Worcestershire Beacon (425m/1395ft).
10. The Brecon Beacons. Highpoint: Pen y Fan (886m/2907ft).

20 BRITISH ISLAND HIGHPOINTS

1. Cliff top (off Northumberland) — (d) Inner Farne
2. Hautnez — (c) Guernsey
3. Holyhead Mountain — (b) Anglesey
4. Le Moulin — (i) Sark
5. Le Rond — (a) Alderney
6. Snaefell — (e) Isle of Man
7. St. Boniface Down — (g) Isle of Wight
8. The Mount — (f) Isle of Sheppey
9. Unnamed (in Scilly Isles) — (k) St Mary's
10. Unnamed (off Devon north) — (h) Lundy
11. Unnamed (off Devon south) — (l) Thatcher Rock
12. Unnamed (off Pembrokeshire) — (j) Skomer

21 LAKE DISTRICT: ODD ONE OUT

1. They are all tarns, e.g. Boo Tarn, except Black, which does not exist.
2. They are all Pikes, e.g. Causey Pike, except Rosthwaite, which is a Fell.
3. They are all High, e.g. High Knott, except High Road, which does not exist.
4. They are all Great, e.g. Great End, except The Band, which is a ridge of Bowfell.
5. They are all features on Scafell, except Jack's Rake, which is on Pavey Ark, Langdale.
6. Whinlatter Pass is the only one with a road over it.
7. Hayeswater is the only one that is not a reservoir.
8. Wet Side Edge is the only one whose negotiation does not involve scrambling.
9. They are all Bottoms except Long, which is a Top.
10. They are all crags on Scafell Pike except Walla Crag, which is by Derwent Water.

22 LAKE DISTRICT HILLS: ANAGRAMS

1. Great Gable.
2. Blencathra.
3. Wetherlam.
4. Robinson.
5. Harter Fell.
6. Dollywaggon Pike.
7. Scafell Pike.
8. High Street.
9. Harrison Stickle.
10. Haystacks.
11. Coniston Old Man.
12. Yewbarrow.
13. Whiteside.
14. Lingmell.
15. Black Combe.

23 EUROPE: HITTING THE HIGH SPOTS

1. Botrange   (b)   Belgium
2. Carrantuohil   (f)   Ireland
3. Gerlach   (k)   Slovakia
4. Grossglockner   (a)   Austria
5. Kékes   (e)   Hungary
6. Knieff   (g)   Luxembourg.

   Knieff is 1m higher than Bourgplatz, which was considered to be the highest point prior to re-measurement by GPS satellite in 1994.

7. Moldoveaunu   (j)   Romania
8. Møllehøj   (c)   Denmark
9. Mulhacen   (l)   Spain
10. Rysy   (i)   Poland
11. Vaalserberg   (h)   Netherlands
12. Zugspitze   (d)   Germany

24 EUROPEAN MOUNTAIN RANGES

1. The Pyrenees, on the border of France and Spain.
2. The Jotunheimen.
3. (b) The Pindus Mountains of north Greece. The Rhodope Mountains are more extensive but most of the range is in Bulgaria rather than Greece. The White Mountains are a smaller range in western Crete.
4. The Picos de Europa.
5. The Tatras.
6. (b) The Jura mountains. Highpoint: Le Crêt de la Neige (1720m/5643ft). The Vosges mountains are further north, while the Cévennes are in south-central France.
7. The Appenines.
8. (b) The Sierra de Guadarrama, c.35ml north of Madrid. The Sierra de Gredos is c.85ml west of Madrid, while the Sierra Nevada is in the south of Spain.
9. (a) The Gennargentu Massif, Sardinia.
10. The Ardennes, situated mainly in Belgium and Luxembourg.

25 IRELAND & NORTHERN IRELAND

1. Carrauntoohil (1039m/3408ft) in County Kerry.
2. (a) Macgillicuddy's Reeks.
3. (b) Using a prominence criterion of 15m/50ft, there are 14 'Irish Munros'. If a prominence criterion of 30m/100ft is used, the number is reduced to 13.
4. Slieve Donard (850m/2790ft) in County Down.
5. (c) Purple Mountain. According to Samuel Lewis' The Topographical Dictionary of Ireland (1837), it derives its name from 'the colour of the shivered slate on its surface'.
6. The Mourne Wall is a substantial stone wall built to define the perimeter of the Belfast Water Commission catchment area in the Mourne Mountains. It runs over 15 mountains/hills, including the top of Slieve Donard.
7. (c) The Wicklow Mountains, County Wicklow. Highest peak: Lugnaquilla (925m/3035ft).
8. (a) Croaghaun, Achill Island. The cliffs at Slieve League are 601m/1972ft high. The cliffs at Moher are 214m/702ft high.
9. (b) Croagh Patrick, County Mayo. According to legend, St Patrick fasted on the summit for 40 days in the 5th century. Some pilgrims make the ascent barefoot.
10. (a) Arderin.

26 THE EUROPEAN ALPS

1. An alp is a grassy high mountain pasture below the snowline where animals are taken to feed in summer.
2. (b) 82. If a prominence criterion of 100m (of summit above surroundings) is applied, the list is reduced to 52. If a prominence criterion of 500m is applied, the list is reduced to 22.
3. (c) Switzerland. Exact numbers per country are complicated by peaks on the borders between countries, but Switzerland has the most.
4. (b) 1786, on August 8. The ascent was made without ropes or ice axes, and to collect a reward of twenty thalers (silver coins) that had been offered twenty-five years previously.
5. (b) By the firing of cannons.

6. (b) 1854–1865. The period runs from the first ascent of the Wetterhorn in 1854 to the first ascent of the Matterhorn in 1865.

7. (c) Mittellegi (NE Ridge). This is on the Eiger. The NE Ridge of the Matterhorn is known as the Hörnli Ridge.

8. The Eiger (Ogre), the Mönch (Monk) or the Jungfrau (Maiden or Virgin). The rack-and-cog railway climbs through the Eiger to the Jungfraugoch, a 3454m/11,332ft col between the Jungfrau and the Mönch.

9. The Aiguille du Midi (3842m/12,605ft). When it was opened in 1955 it was the highest cable car in the world. The record was broken in 1960 by the cable car up Pico Espejo (Mirror Peak, 4765m/15,633ft), above the city of Merida in the Venezuelan Andes. The Aiguille du Midi cable car still holds the record for the most vertical ascent, from 1035m in Chamonix to 3842m at the summit.

10. The Haute Route (High Route) is a 110ml/177km hut-to-hut hiking route over high mountain passes, linking the Alpine centres of Chamonix (Mont Blanc) and Zermatt (The Matterhorn). It began as a mountaineering route developed by British mountaineers in the mid-nineteenth century. The term is now also sometimes applied to other long-distance hut-to-hut routes.

27 HIGH COUNTRY

1. (b) Nepal (eight). Pakistan has five. India has none. The 14th (lowest) 8000m peak is in Tibet, incorporated into China since 1950. Many of the 8000m peaks in Nepal and Pakistan are also on the border of Tibet and China.

2. Austria (three), France, Switzerland, UK (two each), others (one each).

3. New Zealand.

4. (a) Burundi. The highest mountain in Burundi is Mount Heha (2685m/8809ft). The highest mountain in Cameroon is Mount Cameroon (4095m/13,435ft). The highest mountain in Kenya is Mount Kenya (5199m/17/057ft).

5. Spain. The highest mountain is Mount Teide (3718m/12,198ft) on Tenerife in the Canary Islands, off the coast of Africa. The highest mountain on the mainland is Mulhacen (3478m/11,411ft).

6. (a) Bolivia. Colombia and Ecuador have Pacific coastlines.

7. Andorra. The lowest point of this mountainous country is the point at which the largest river (the Gran Valira) crosses the border to flow south into Spain.

8. New Guinea.

9. (b) Norway. The highest mountain is Galdhöpiggen (2469m/8100ft). The highest point of solid rock on nearby Glittertind (2452m/8045ft) is covered by an ice cap. For much of the 20th century the ice exceeded 17m in thickness, so making Glittertind the highest mountain. The ice cap is now only 10–15m thick, making Glittertind a few metres lower than Galdhöpiggen. In Sweden, on the highest mountain Kebnekaise, the higher, glaciated south top may similarly become lower than the rocky, ice-free north top, although in 2012 it grew by 2.1m to 2101.8m/6896ft. Watch this space.

10. (c) Canada (Ellesmere Island).

28 MOUNTAINS OF THE WORLD

1. Mount Fuji, Japan.

2. Kilimanjaro (5895m/19,341ft), Tanzania.

3. Alpamayo, Peru.

4. (a) Mount Alberta.

5. Mount Vinson.

6. Mount Olympus, Greece.

7. (a) Huascaran.

8. Table Mountain.

9. Lenin Peak, on the border of Tajikistan and Kyrgyzstan. Before 1928 it was known as Mount Kaufman (after the first governor of Turkestan), but for most of the 20th Century, as part of the Soviet Union, it was called Pik Lenin (Lenin Peak). Since the fall of the Soviet Union some now call it Mount Kaufman again. In 2006 the now independent country of Tajikistan renamed it Abu Ali ibni Sino (Avicenna Peak), while in Kyrgyzstan it is now called Pik Sary Tash.

10. (c) Nanda Devi. The Hindi name means Blessed Goddess.

29 MOUNTAIN RANGES OF THE WORLD

1. The Andes.
2. (b) The Karakoram.
3. The Atlas.
4. (b) The Coast Range.
5. The Caucasus.
6. (b) The Ruwenzori.
7. (a) The Sierra Madre.
8. (b) The Pamirs. The highest mountain was named Stalin Peak when it was discovered in 1933 and re-named Communism Peak in 1962. It is the highest mountain in Tajikistan and, following the fall of the Soviet Union, was re-named Ismoil Somoni in 1998, after the ruler of an ancient Persian dynasty.
9. (c) The Great Dividing Range. The Blue Mountains are part of this range.
10. (c) The Taurus. Some sources list higher mountains than Demirkazik, but geographically these lie outside the Taurus.

30 ALPS OF THE WORLD

1. Alpes Montes   (k)   The moon
2. Bavarian Alps   (c)   Germany
3. Bernese Alps   (j)   Switzerland
4. Chuya Alps   (h)   Siberia (Russia)
5. Julian Alps   (i)   Slovenia
6. Kita Alps   (e)   Japan
7. Maritime Alps   (b)   France
8. Southern Alps   (f)   New Zealand
9. Staunings Alps   (d)   Greenland
10. Stubai Alps   (a)   Austria
11. Transylvanian Alps (g) Romania
12. Trinity Alps   (l)   USA

31 THE USA

1. (b) 17.
2. (b) Colorado. Alaska's average elevation is c.580m/1900ft. Montana's is c.1040m/3400ft.
3. (b) Colorado, which is generally regarded as having 54 fourteeners, depending on the criterion used. California is generally regarded as having 13. Montana has none.
4. The Appalachian Trail.
5. (c) 5500m/18,000ft.
6. (a) Grand Canyon.
7. (b) Yellowstone.
8. (a) Mount Elbert (4401m/14,440ft). Mount Rainier is 4392m/14,411ft. Mount Shasta is 4322m/14,179ft.
9. (b) Florida. Florida's highpoint is Britton Hill (105/345ft), Delaware's is a roadside marker (136m/447ft), Louisiana's is Driskill Mountain (163m/535ft).
10. The Sierra Nevada.

32 THE NUMBERS GAME

1. The Empty Quarter
2. Zero Gully.
3. Half Dome.
4. Two Tier Buttress.
5. The Three Sisters.
6. The Five Sisters.
7. The Seven Sisters.
8. The Twelve Bens.
9. Twenty Years on Ben Nevis.
10. Les Plus Belles 100 Courses.
11. The Valley of 1000 Falls.
12. The Valley of 10,000 Smokes.

33 LONG DISTANCE TRAILS OF ENGLAND & WALES

1. (c) The South West Coast Path, formed from the amalgamation of the Somerset & North Devon, Cornwall, South Devon and Dorset Coastal Paths.
2. The Lyke Wake Walk.
3. The Weavers Way. Cloth making was once a major local industry.
4. (c) Offa's Dyke Path. Offa's Dyke was a large earthwork that separated Wales from Mercia (the modern English Midlands). It is traditionally attributed to Offa, an eight century King of Mercia.
5. The Pennine Way.
6. (b) Sheffield Country Walk.
7. The Pembrokeshire Coast Path. In 2012 it was joined with other Welsh coastal paths to form the 870ml/1400km Wales Coast Path.
8. (c) The Viking Way.
9. Dartmoor and Exmoor in Devon.
10. (d) The Trent.

34 CAMPING

1. A geodesic tent is a dome-shaped tent whose poles intersect to form triangular and hexagonal panels, producing a strong tent with a high internal volume.
2. A flysheet traps insulating dead-air between inner tent and flysheet.
3. If the tent frame is attached to the flysheet, the inner tent can be pitched and dismantled dry in wet weather.
4. (b) A light-coloured tent is warmest. Dark colours radiate heat more readily at night, while a mesh tent traps no heat.
5. A dunnel is a cross between a dome and a tunnel, combining the internal space of a dome with the aerodynamic qualities of a tunnel.
6. An unattached flysheet should have a smaller footprint than the tent, so that condensation from tent walls does not drip onto it.
7. A sleeping bag does not increase the warmth of its occupant. It can only maintain its occupant's warmth for a certain amount of time.

8. (b) The warmest place to camp is on a hillside. Hill tops are colder because they are higher and more open to the elements. Depressions are colder because cold night air flows downhill into them.

9. Snowmelt should be collected at night because it freezes overnight.

10. (c) The tent wall was made from multiple layers of fabric, which created insulating dead-air spaces between them.

35 BRITISH MOUNTAIN RIDGES

1. Bristly Ridge   (g)   Glyder Fach
2. Curved Ridge   (d)   Buachaille Etive Mor
3. Devil's Ridge   (j)   Sgurr a' Mhaim
4. Fiacaill Ridge   (e)   Cairn Lochan
5. Forcan Ridge   (k)   The Saddle
6. Lancet Edge   (i)   Sgor Iutharn
7. Long Leachas   (a)   Ben Alder
8. Pinnacle Ridge   (f)   Crib Goch
9. Sentries' Ridge   (h)   Mynnyd Mawr
10. Sharp Edge   (c)   Blencathra or The Saddleback
11. Steel Edge   (l)   Wetherlam
12. Tower Ridge   (b)   Ben Nevis

36 FAMOUS BRITISH MOUNTAINEERS

1. Joe Simpson (1960–).
2. Tom Patey (1932–70).
3. Edward Whymper (1840–1911).
4. Harold (Bill) Tilman (1898–1977).
5. Joe Brown (1930–).
6. Alfred Mummery (1855–95).
7. Chris Bonington (1934–).
8. Geoffrey Winthrop Young (1876–1958).
9. William Slingsby (1849–1929).
10. Julie Tullis (1939–86).

37 IT'S COLD OUTSIDE

1. The process of vasoconstriction constricts blood vessels in the extremities. This reduces blood flow to the fingers and toes, allowing the flow of heated blood to be diverted to the body's core.

2. To prevent heat loss through the head, even though scientists have debunked the old myth that more heat is lost through the head than through other parts of the body. The myth may derive from US army experiments on subjects who wore covering on every part of the body except the head. Nevertheless, the head, including the face, is usually the least covered part of the body in cold weather. Covering it will reduce overall heat loss, especially as vasoconstriction does not work in the head (fortunately!).

3. The best insulation from the cold is (b) a vacuum. The next best insulation is (a) a still gas (e.g. air).

4. Loose clothes are warmer because they can trap warm air next to the skin.

5. (c) 3–5 minutes.

6. Mittens. By separating the fingers, gloves increase the area of exposed skin and therefore the amount of heat loss. Mittens also enable warm air to be trapped between the fingers.

7. (a) Sintering is the process by which snow crystals bond together to form a firmer, compact mass. It occurs when individual snow crystals lose their angular shape (e.g. by wind action, melting, shovelling and other forms of compression) and freeze together into a more cohesive structure. It is the process by which snow compacts when stamped on and the process by which snowballs are made.

8. Alcohol dilates (opens) blood vessels, thereby increasing blood flow and heat loss by a process of vasodilatation opposite to that of vasoconstriction (see Answer 1).

9. (a) Down. It also has the least weight and is the most compressible.

10. The earth is closer to the sun in winter than in summer, but it has a 23.5° tilt. In a northern winter the northern hemisphere is tilted away from the sun and receives less direct solar rays, which have further to travel through the atmosphere. The reverse is true in the southern hemisphere.

38 GLACIERS

1. Greenland.
2. A crevasse is formed when a glacier flows over a rise or down a drop, causing its surface to stretch and crack open.
3. (c) The Hubbard Glacier, Alaska, USA. The Baltoro Glacier is c.39ml/ 62km long. The Athabasca Glacier is c.4ml/6km long. The world's longest glacier is the Lambert-Fisher (c.320ml/514km) in Antarctica.
4. A dry glacier is one whose surface is not covered by snow and whose crevasses are easily seen.
5. A *bergschrund* is a large crevasse at the head of a glacier that separates flowing ice from stagnant ice or rock above.
6. (c) A glacier table is a mushroom-like glacial feature formed by a rock lying on top of an ice column, which has been protected from the sun's rays while all the surrounding ice has melted.
7. They would abseil from it. An ice bollard is a 'mushroom' of ice cut into an ice surface with the aid of an ice axe for use as an abseil anchor.
8. (c) 20m/65ft. Between 1992 and 2003 the glacier's speed of movement varied from 5700m to 12,600m per year.
9. A nunatak is an isolated mountain peak that projects through the surface of an ice cap.
10. (c) Iceberg movement in the North Atlantic.

39 MOUNTAIN WEATHER

1. When wind flows across a mountain, it cools as it rises on the near (windward) side, causing water vapour in the air to condense and fall as rain. A rain shadow is a region of less rain on the far (leeward) side, where descending, warming air causes clouds to break up.

2. (b) 8 (gale: 39–46mph/62–74kph).

    Full Beaufort wind scale:

0	Calm	Below 1mph/1kph
1	Light air	1–3mph/1–5kph
2	Light breeze	4–7mph/6–11kph
3	Gentle breeze	8–12mph/12–19kph
4	Moderate breeze	13–18mph/20–28kph
5	Fresh breeze	19–24mph/29–38kph
6	Strong breeze	25–31mph/39–49kph
7	Near gale	32–38mph/50–61kph
8	Gale	39–46mph/62–74kph
9	Severe gale	47–54mph/75–88kph
10	Storm	55–63mph/89–102kph
11	Violent storm	64–73mph/103–117kph
12–17	Hurricane	Over 73mph/117kph

3. Katabatic winds are cold, gravity-induced winds that flow off mountains into valleys, especially on cold nights. The term 'katabatic' comes from the Greek and means 'descending'.

4. (c) Mount Washington, New Hampshire. The wind speed was recorded at the summit observatory at an elevation of 1197m/6288ft on 12 April 1934.

5. (a) Mount Baker, Washington, measured at an elevation of 1300m/4300ft. Mount Rainier held the record for many years, when 28,511mm/1122.5ins of snow fell between 19 February 1971, and 18 February 1972, at Paradise Ranger Station at an elevation of 1650m/5400ft. Mount Baker broke the record between 1 July 1998, and 30 June 1999 (now the official snowfall measuring season).

6. (b) 2°C/3.6°F. In moist air, on a cloudy or humid day, this decrease is almost halved, because condensing water vapour in rising air releases energy in the form of heat (see Answer 1).

7. A glory is a haloed shadow of a person's head cast deep into mist by the sun. It is most often seen when walking along a mountain ridge above cloud.

8. (a) Latitude. At high latitudes, towards the North and South Poles (latitude 90°), temperatures are lower. At low latitudes, towards the Equator (latitude 0°), temperatures are higher.

9. A cloud cap on a mountain appears stationery even in a strong wind because cloud continually forms at the windward edge and breaks up at the leeward edge (see Answer 1).

10. (c) -9°C/15.8°F. The human body loses heat through conduction, convection, evaporation and radiation. This heat warms an insulating layer of air next to the skin, but this is blown away by wind. The higher the wind speed, and the lower the air temperature, the greater the wind chill as the body tries to compensate for heat loss. Formulae for the calculation of wind chill vary historically and geographically. This is due to the number of measurement variables involved, e.g. face v whole body measurement, naked v clothed measurement. In 2001, Canada, the UK and the USA agreed a new formula. This and wind chill charts are freely available on the internet.

40 MOUNTAIN FLORA & FAUNA

1. The dog.

2. (a) The Cairngorms.

3. (a) The Cairngorms. Scrub trees grow to a height of over 600m/2000ft on the eastern hillsides of Glen Feshie.

4. The north and south facing slopes of a mountain support different flora because they receive different amounts of sunshine. In the northern hemisphere the south facing slopes receive more sunshine, and vice versa in the southern hemisphere.

5. (b) The white-tailed eagle or sea eagle.

6. The adder.

7. (a) Ice worms.

8. High mountain plants have waxy leaves to reduce water loss by evaporation.

9. (c) 37,000ft (11,277m). A Ruppell's Vulture collided with an aircraft at this altitude in 1973. The bird was identified by its feather remains.

10. The edelweiss.

41 LITERARY CONNECTIONS

1. (a) Kilimanjaro. The story was called *The Snows of Kilimanjaro*.
2. (b) *The Magic Mountain (Der Zauberberg)*.
3. (a) The Alpine Journal, published by the (British) Alpine Club. The Cairngorm Club Journal was founded in 1893. The Scottish Mountaineering Club Journal was founded in 1889.
4. (c) The Matterhorn, a 3745m/12,279ft peak on the northern boundary of Yosemite.
5. (c) Roraima (2875m/9433ft) in Monte Roraima National Park on the Venezuelan border with Brazil and Guyana. Pico Cristobal Colon (Spanish for Christopher Columbus) and Pico Simon Bolivar are 5700m/18,700ft mountains in Columbia.
6. (Sherpa) Tenzing Norgay.
7. (c) Rum Doodle. The book was *The Ascent of Rum Doodle*.
8. (c) Mount Kenya. The book was *No Picnic on Mount Kenya*.
9. (d) Algernon Swinburne (1837–1909). During various alcoholic adventures, he climbed Bla Bheinn with John Nichol, Professor of English at Glasgow University.
10. (a) Lord Byron (1788–1824). He scrambled up Lochnagar with a club foot via the prow of The Stuic.

42 FILMS

1. *The Eiger Sanction*.
2. Mount Rushmore, South Dakota, USA.
3. (c) K2, Pakistan.
4. The Andes.
5. (b) He is killed by rockfall.
6. *Picnic at Hanging Rock*.
7. *Cliffhanger*.
8. (b) Stromboli.
9. *Mission: Impossible 2*.
10. The Sierra Madre. The film is *Treasure of the Sierra Madre*.
11. (b) El Capitan in Yosemite National Park, California, USA.
12. *The Spy Who Loved Me*.

43 POT POURRI 1

1. Ben Nevis, which won the Grand National in 1980.
2. (c) 25%.
3. The Ptarmigan Restaurant (1097m/3600ft) at the top station of the funicular railway, Cairn Gorm.
4. (b) 1974.
5. Ice axes and crampons were used to climb the soft chalk.
6. In the Tasman Sea, 435ml/700km off the coast of Australia.
7. Landing on the rock is now prohibited by international agreement through UNESCO.
8. (c) 2801m/9186ft.
9. The 1980s. The event began in 1980 and cyclists have been allowed to compete since 1985. The first cyclist to win was Tim Gould on a mountain bike in 1989. In the history of the event, runners have beaten horses twice only.
10. (b) Le Crêt de la Neige (5643ft/1720m), Jura, France.

44 POT POURRI 2

1. The ordnance is the department of the army that deals with supplies. Following the defeat of the Jacobite army at the Battle of Culloden in 1746, it became responsible for road surveying during the government occupation of the Scottish Highlands.
2. (c) Tasmania, Australia. The name of the Scottish national park that includes the Munro Ben Lomond is Ben Lomond and The Trossachs National Park.
3. Cross-country skiing. *Langlauf* is the European term.
4. (b) Crag Hill (839m/2752ft).
5. Climbing boots. Hut shoes/slippers may be provided.
6. (b) 8700m/28,500ft.
7. A Tyrolean Traverse is a method of crossing a gap or chasm. The climber pulls himself/herself along a rope stretched across the gap.
8. (b) Massachusetts, USA.
9. Inuit (Eskimo).
10. (a) 'Balls to you, Sir John'.

45 POT POURRI 3

1. Nepal: Sagarmatha (Everest) National Park, created in 1976.
2. (a) £6.
3. He jumped into the volcanic crater of Mount Etna, Italy.
4. (b) Napes Needle, Great Gable, Lake District.
5. The 1970s. Japanese mountaineer Junko Tabei reached the summit in 1975.
6. (a) The Ben Nevis race.
7. A double sheet bend is a knot used to join ropes of different thicknesses.
8. (a) An abseiling accident. It is thought that the pinnacle to which his rope was attached broke. Alternatively, he may have leant against a boulder that gave way. As there were no witnesses, there are other explanations and conspiracy theories.
9. (a) Modern avalanche control began in the Dolomites in World War One, when Alpine troops used shellfire to trigger avalanches on the enemy.
10. There is no world governing body of mountaineering.

46 POT POURRI 4

1. Sugar lumps.
2. (b) 1968.
3. Triple Divide Mountain divides the catchment areas of streams that flow to three different destinations: the Atlantic Ocean, the Pacific Ocean and Hudson's Bay.
4. (a) 1951. Lesotho is the only independent country in the world that lies entirely above 1000m/3300ft.
5. He thought they were carried there by pilgrims.
6. Sedimentary rocks are formed from the shells and skeletons of sea animals, which are deposited on the sea bed and uplifted.

7. (b) 9 thousand million. Although each pore is c.20,000 times smaller than a drop of water, it is 700 times bigger than a molecule of water vapour (a gas), allowing sweat, for example, to pass through it. The Goretex membrane is only micrometres thick (a micrometre is one thousandth of a millimetre), which is why it has to be laminated to other material to form a garment.

8. They thought that using crampons was cheating.

9. (c) 6557. 37 of these were at an elevation of 1000m or over. Visiting remaining trig points (trigpointing) has developed into a new pursuit.

10. (c) On the moon.

47 POT POURRI 5

1. French.

2. (b) Motor cycles.

3. River valleys are normally eroded by rivers into a V-shape, unless a glacier grinds them down and carves them into a U-shape.

4. (a) Luigi, Duke of the Abruzzi. He thought K2 was too difficult ever to be climbed, but the standard route is today named the Abruzzi Spur in his honour.

5. On 14 December 1991, Mount Cook lost 10m of height from its summit when a massive rock avalanche caused an earthquake that measured 3.9 on the Richter scale.

6. (c) 10–20 years.

7. Eat it. *Bergstiegeressen* is an inexpensive dish that guardians of German and Austrian Alpine huts are required to provide on the menu for poor climbers.

8. (c) Porridge oats.

9. A butte is smaller than a mesa. A mesa is a tableland, formed when an upper layer of hard rock protects a lower level of softer rock from erosion. A butte is an eroded mesa. Precise definitions vary but, in normal geographical usage, a mesa's top is wider than its height, while a butte's top is smaller. The world's most spectacular buttes, made famous by John Ford westerns, are found in Monument Valley, Utah, USA.

10. (c) On the moon.

48 POT POURRI 6

1. 'K' is an abbreviation of 'Karakoram'.

2. (a) The Dead Sea, Israel (-422m/1385ft, although this varies). Badwater Basin in Death Valley is -85m/280ft. The Qattara Depression is -133m/436ft.

3. An igloo. Another type of dome, called a Quinzhee in Canada, can be built by compacting snow then hollowing it out, but it is unlikely to last.

4. (a) Hypsometry, also known as hypsography, is the measurement of height.

5. Limpets.

6. (a) Leonardo da Vinci (1452–1519).

7. The highest sea cliffs in Europe are at Hornelen in Norway. The second highest sea cliffs in Europe are at Cape Enniberg (754m/2473ft) in the Faroe Islands.

8. (c) The highest sea cliffs in the world are on the Kalaupapa Peninsula on the island of Molokai, Hawaii, USA. The height given for the cliffs varies considerably but, if the steep-sided fjord peaks of New Zealand are excluded, they remain the highest in the world.

9. The more food carried, the heavier the pack, and the more energy expended in carrying it.

10. (c) Surface height reached. Owing to their landing site, they reached a height of c.7830m/(25,700ft).

49 POT POURRI 7

1. (b) Maldives highpoint: 2m/8ft. Bahamas highpoint: 63m/207ft. Seychelles highpoint: 905m/2969ft.

2. He paraglided from near the summit (8848m/29,029ft) to Camp 2 at 5900m/19,400ft.

3. (b) 200,000 years.

4. La Montagne was the name of the extreme democratic party, whose leaders included Danton and Robespierre.

5. (b) Chimborazo.

6. (a) The Refugio Independencia is situated at 6546m/21,477ft on Aconcagua, Argentina.
7. Nowhere.
8. Faulting, volcanic eruption (producing cone-shaped mountains), underground volcanic intrusion (producing dome-shaped mountains).
9. (b) Oregano.
10. The planet is regarded as a perfect sphere with a fixed diameter, and heights are measured relative to that. When measuring lunar heights the moon is regarded as a perfect sphere with a diameter of 1080ml/1738km.

50 POT POURRI 8

1. (a) 1492. The climb was made by royal decree when King Charles VIII of France ordered that Mont Aiguille be climbed. Antoine de Ville de Dompjulien, one of his servants, obliged. The climb was made using ladders, ropes and other artificial aids. The summit was not reached again until 1834.
2. Canoeing.
3. (a) Top of the World Provincial Park is located in the Kootenay Range of the Rocky Mountains in British Columbia, Canada.
4. Andinismo is the Andean equivalent of Alpinism.
5. (c) Nuts. Chocolate and a jam sandwich will give a quicker energy fix, but nuts have more protein, which releases energy more slowly than sugars and carbohydrates.
6. Women were first allowed to climb Mount Fuji during the Meiji period in the late nineteenth century (1868–1912). The first known ascent was by a monk in 663. The first known Westerner to climb Fuji was Sir Rutherford Alcock in 1868. The first known Western woman to climb it was Lady Fanny Parkes in 1869.
7. (b) 58. Seeking the 'apex of America', she misjudged Huascaran's altitude in a snowstorm and believed she had climbed a 7300m peak. In fact she had climbed the 6648m/21,812ft south peak. The higher 6768m/22,205ft north peak was not climbed until 1932.

8. In fluid dynamics, a Karman Vortex Street is a set of swirling vortices formed when a fluid separates to flow around an object. On mountains it is the alternating clockwise and anti-clockwise eddies of strong wind formed in the lee of a mountain when the wind divides to pass around it. One of the world's largest Karman Vortex Streets is formed in the lee of Hallasan Volcano, South Korea, every winter.

9. The Bungle Bungles are a range of beehive-shaped sandstone formations in Purnululu National Park, Western Australia.

10. Yes!

Luath Press Limited
committed to publishing well written books worth reading

LUATH PRESS takes its name from Robert Burns, whose little collie Luath (*Gael.,* swift or nimble) tripped up Jean Armour at a wedding and gave him the chance to speak to the woman who was to be his wife and the abiding love of his life. Burns called one of 'The Twa Dogs' Luath after Cuchullin's hunting dog in Ossian's *Fingal*. Luath Press was established in 1981 in the heart of Burns country, and now resides a few steps up the road from Burns' first lodgings on Edinburgh's Royal Mile.
Luath offers you distinctive writing with a hint of unexpected pleasures.

Most bookshops in the UK, the US, Canada, Australia, New Zealand and parts of Europe either carry our books in stock or can order them for you. To order direct from us, please send a £sterling cheque, postal order, international money order or your credit card details (number, address of cardholder and expiry date) to us at the address below. Please add post and packing as follows: UK – £1.00 per delivery address; overseas surface mail – £2.50 per delivery address; overseas airmail – £3.50 for the first book to each delivery address, plus £1.00 for each additional book by airmail to the same address. If your order is a gift, we will happily enclose your card or message at no extra charge.

Luath Press Limited
543/2 Castlehill
The Royal Mile
Edinburgh EH1 2ND
Scotland

Telephone: 0131 225 4326 (24 hours)
Fax: 0131 225 4324
email: sales@luath.co.uk
Website: www.luath.co.uk